They Didn't Know

My Personal Journey with Lyme Disease

by Martha M. Conan

The contents of this work, including, but not limited to, the accuracy of events, people, and places depicted; opinions expressed; permission to use previously published materials included; and any advice given or actions advocated are solely the responsibility of the author, who assumes all liability for said work and indemnifies the publisher against any claims stemming from publication of the work.

All Rights Reserved
Copyright © 2019 by Martha M. Conan

No part of this book may be reproduced or transmitted, downloaded, distributed, reverse engineered, or stored in or introduced into any information storage and retrieval system, in any form or by any means, including photocopying and recording, whether electronic or mechanical, now known or hereinafter invented without permission in writing from the publisher.

Dorrance Publishing Co
585 Alpha Drive
Pittsburgh, PA 15238
Visit our website at *www.dorrancebookstore.com*

ISBN: 978-1-4809-9268-9
eISBN: 978-1-4809-9186-6

Dedication

I would like to dedicate this book to all individuals throughout the world who are suffering from Lyme disease, those who are misdiagnosed without knowing they were sick and for the physicians and practitioners who treat us. May this book be a path toward liberation to knowing that Lyme patients, their caregivers, and doctors are not alone in their fight for a cure.

Acknowledgements

This book would not be possible without the knowledge and patience of the Lyme disease treatment team: Dr. Eboni Cornish, Dr. Ronald Stram, Jennifer Goldstock, Dr. Daniel Cameron, Arthur Smuckler, Mary Kay Gillis, Karen Dellas, Kyle Carleo, Pete Haley, Martin Canavan, the nursing and secretary staffs of the Shor Center and Stram Center. I am grateful to Stacy Carey, The Conan family: Tim, Mairead, Mack, Mary Kate, and Maura Clare, Cindy Harrigan, Laurie Tebbe, Mary Hanus, Eva Haughie, Debi Collins, Marilyn Anderson, Kim Mulvahill, Shelly Dodge, Jill Ennis, Ed Eagan, Father Billy Clark, Father Fred Manara, Evie Gates, Linda Hook, Gregg Kirk, and Neil McCurn, Esq., all who have encouraged and engaged in helping me maintain my independence by taking me shopping, doctors appointments and on trips. These individuals also provide me with continuous spiritual and emotional guidance. It is also important to note the ongoing support from my personal trainers at Elevate Fitness and Edge Fitness who go out their way to prepare specialized trainings to meet my functional exercise needs. I would also like to express my ongoing thanks to all those who help me with prompting me to write my story (Art Smukler), editor (Margot Jacoby), photographer (Laura Marino) and publisher (Dorrance Publishing Company) . Most importantly, I would like to thank God for his unconditional love and heavenly support as I walk the path to recovery.

Foreword

In 2003 I started having strange neurological symptoms such as foot drop, lower extremity weakness and pain, inability to feel the bottom of my feet, and otherwise, horrific zaps of pain. During the next few years I had developed insomnia, depression, chronic fatigue, migrating pain, chronic migraines, ataxia, aphasia, and severe back and leg pain. All the while, I worked thirty to forty hours per week and attended graduate school full time. However, I started tripping and falling at work and school and had difficulty with my memory. The end result was for me to stop work and quit school. I saw a spinal doctor, Dr. Stephen Robinson, and a primary care physician, Dr. Carl Butch, for bulging discs, spinal stenosis, back and leg pain, and neuropathy. Dr. Robinson referred me to the spinal clinic's pain clinic where I received spinal injections for pain. None of the cortisone injections relieved pain for more than a day and other pain medications provided no relief. I was given a possible diagnosis of either MS or ALS. Finally, Dr. Robinson referred me to Dr. Antonio Marasegan, a neurologist, to test me for an upper motor neuron disease, which is a primary indicator of MS and ALS. He could not find any evidence of either disease and had no idea what caused my problems. In July, 2012, I was referred to Dr. Eboni Cornish, a Lyme-Literate physician in Virginia, who diagnosed me with Lyme disease and with co-infections Babesia, Bartonella, and Ehrlicia and started me on a treatment plan. My mind was getting a little clearer and I could function a little better, but my physical issues developed into peripheral neuropathy. Since 2009 I have had to use a cane and double walking sticks. Presently, I use a walker for short distances and a wheelchair for long ones. My present Lyme nurse practioner, Jennifer Goldstock, manages my treatment. I still seek alternative, holistic, and conventional medical advice and treatment for this horrific disease. It is life changing and it has changed my life and has given me a cause to let others know that this is a most difficult disease to diagnose and treat. This proves that with proper clinical diagnosis, Lyme disease can be identified and properly treated.

Contents

Part One. 1
Mike's Bikes 3
Birth of the Honeydew 5
Christmas 1972 9
May 1980 11
"I Wasn't Hungry". 13
My Roaring Twenties 15
The Starter Marriage 17
Dad's Lazyboy 19
Calm Before the Storm 21
Five Element Theory 23
Swiss Cheese Brain 25
Is there a Doctor in the House? 27
A New Chapter 33
Forty-five Minutes. 35
The Aftermath. 39
Acupuncture, Chiropractic, and Physical Therapy – Oh My! 41

Part Two. 43
A Beacon in the Dark 45
The First Day of the Rest of my life: new patient comprehensive evaluation . . . 47

Second Visit: initiation of antibiotics 53
Third Visit: fatigue, ataxia, cerebellar dysfunction. 55
Fourth Visit: conference call. 59
Fifth Visit: severe herx/environmental toxins. 61
Sixth Visit: improved symptoms/pain. 63
Seventh Visit: joint pain/neuropathy 65
Eighth Visit: improved symptoms/ataxia 69
Ninth Visit: detoxification/increased fatigue 71
Tenth Visit: conference call. 73
Eleventh Visit: conference call 75
Twelfth Visit: sleep/digestion 79
Thirteenth Visit: improvement of symptoms/neuropathy 81
Fourteenth Visit: mood instability/ MTHFR. 83
Fifteenth Visit: phone/conference 85
Sixteenth Visit: improved symptoms/dysbiosis. 87

Part 3 91
A New Plan, Stan 93
Here We Go Again 95
Positive. 99
The New Beginning of my Personal Hell 101
Merry Christmas! 105
Zen and the Art of PICC Line Maintenance 107
Phone Consultation. 111
Another Phone Consultation 115
Cruising to Panama. 117
Lyme disease Follow Up 123
Year of the PICC 125
Take a deep Breath and Hold it! 129
What was I Really Doing?. 133
John of God 137
Lyme disease Follow Up 143
"A Separate Reality" 147
Resources. 185

Part One

Chapter One
Mike's Bikes

It was a beautiful sunny day in Chesapeake, Virginia and David and I decided it was great day to go bicycle shopping. We were in our second year of marriage and still in the so-called honeymoon stage. David was a seasoned biker and was always looking for the next best thing when it came to every new endeavor in the biking community. Participating in yearly races and local biking events resulted in him needing repairs or upgrades several times a year.

I was not a professional biker and I rode for fun when I was little. At the age of six, my father slapped white Head skis onto my red ski boots, attached the emergency ski straps, and clicked me into my Cubco bindings; I was suddenly a skier. When Dad first put me on the slopes of the Killington Ski Resort in Vermont, I immediately took to skiing like a fish to water. My entire family skied and since we were Central New Yorkers who loved the winter, snow, and any outside winter sport, it became my favorite outside activity. In September of 2000 when I was thirty-five, I moved to Virginia after I married my husband, who was a Sonar Technician in the US Navy stationed at the Naval Operations Base in Norfolk, Virginia. Then and there I had to get used to warmer weather activities and since my husband biked, I thought I'd try it out.

So it was off to Mike's Bikes, a little bike shop that was very unassuming from the get go, but as you walked through the front door and lobby into the back office, it was magical. The shapes and colors of the shiny metal frames were absolutely incredible for this seasoned skier. Studying art during my high school and college years allowed me to appreciate the beauty of intricate designs, not just in paintings and architecture, but also in functional pieces of equipment, like bicycles.

David was picking out a new helmet and a Camelbak while I was asking Mike many questions about the different types of bikes he had and what the best one for me would be. I knew that I wanted a nice touring ten speed bike in a stylish color of blue or purple. It was also suggested that I also purchase a helmet; I didn't understand why because I never wore a helmet biking or even skiing for that matter, but I bought one that was blue with silver lightning bolts down the sides. So we picked out a nice silver and blue three speed bike for me that had a low crossbar and had to be special ordered.

David suggested that I take it for a test drive and get a feel for the seat, brakes, and handle bars and I agreed. We took it outside to the sidewalk and parking lot and I was all set to try out my new set of wheels! I was so excited to be able to be doing something that my husband loved to do and experience that part of his life with him.

With much anticipation, I grabbed the blue handlebars and swung my right leg over the crossbar and hopped up on the seat. Then I placed my feet on the pedals and prepared to start a new chapter in my life. However, there was a problem. My legs would not move. I was confused and frustrated. David laughed and said, "Just go already, ride. Don't you know how to ride a bike?"

I said, "Of course I do! It's been a while." I was able to pedal a little, but wobbled a lot; I was very unsure of everything. I didn't think much of it, so I ordered the bike and took the helmet home.

This was when life changed and the symptoms started.

Chapter Two
Birth of the Honeydew

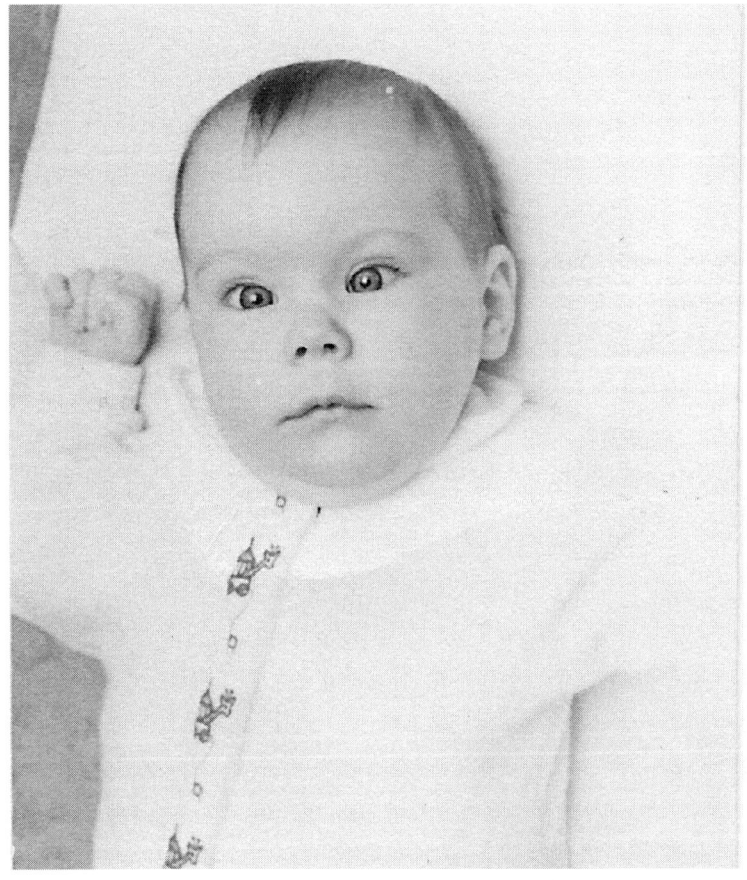

Martha at 7 weeks old

On August 18, 1965 at 3 P.M. in the afternoon in the delivery room of St. Mary's Catholic Hospital in Syracuse, New York, I arrived on this planet kicking and screaming. My birth parents were a young teenage couple who decided to give me up for adoption. I was able to retrieve my birth mother's name, after unearthing an adoption certificate and found she named me, Judith. It is interesting what a person remembers from their youth and how it impacts their life. I do recall being in a large room with many infants and nuns in full habits. There was always something happening, lots of commotion and lots of love. I never felt abandoned.

Dr. Mark and Patricia Conan, were then the parents of three children: Mark, Patricia, and Timothy, and were excited to learn of their approval notification to adopt another child. I was that child. At the age of seven weeks, my new family arrived at St. Mary's Hospital in Syracuse, New York to bring me to my new home. Mark was seventeen at the time and became my Godfather. Patricia, or Patsy as we called her, was ten and Timothy was seven. Patsy was also adopted, unlike Mark and Timothy, who were the spitting image of my parents.

I was raised Catholic. We are an Irish family and I looked the part of the classic "dark Irish" with blue eyes and auburn and tinted-brown hair. Church was, and still is, very important to us and we went every weekend as our hectic schedule permitted. My siblings went to Catholic schools, wore uniforms, and followed the rules of our home and school to a tee until adolescence hit. You see, my parents were older parents, my father being fifty and mother forty-three at the time they adopted me. My 1960s upbringing was more like the 1940s because my parents were old fashioned which are not as present today. It was wonderful. They instilled beautiful values into our lives, like our faith, patriotism, and respect for others and authority.

My father was an Obstetrician Gynecologist who graduated from high school when he was sixteen, college when he was twenty, and medical school three years after that. He was a smart man with an IQ of 150, or so he said. He was born in 1916 on January first and told me the parades and the football games on New Year's Day were designed to celebrate his birthday. Being a naïve girl, I believed him. When I was five years old, he sat me down in a very serious way and told me that I was adopted. I really didn't understand it at the time. At night he would tell me a story of how I came to be in the Conan family. The story goes like this: "Your mother told me to go to the old A & P, a grocery store, to get a honeydew melon. I didn't know which one to get, so I picked some up, squeezed a few, and found one that was pink, warm, and fuzzy and it was YOU! I put you in a brown paper bag and you were the best honeydew melon we ever had."

Now, mind you, my sister, who was also adopted, has olive skin and dark eyes, and was a papoose from the Onondaga Reservation left on the doorstep.

My mom was an incredible mother. She was a social worker who worked with children and specialized in foster care and adoption. Since Dad worked day and night with patient appointments and deliveries, Mom decided to stay at home and raise her children. Many times she was not only the mom, but the dad too. She had the patience of all the angels in heaven keeping our house neat and tidy and handling four children. When I was young I asked her how she met my father and she told me that she followed a redheaded boy home from Mass every Sunday when she was little, but never knew who he was. She then shared that when Dad came home from his duty in the military, his mother suggested that he call that nice Pat Eagan. He asked her out on a date. That's when they fell in love and got married within a year. They were married for fifty-seven years when Dad passed away.

Mark and Patsy attended grammar school at the Church of the Most Holy Rosary. Tim and I attended St. Ann's School, a smaller sister school to Most Holy Rosary. Mom ran St. Ann's Grammar School Library and it suited her well because she could keep an eye on her two youngest children. Patsy continued her high school education at Rosary while Tim and Mark went on to Christian Brothers Academy, and I went to Bishop Ludden High School.

All was well when I young. Mark taught me how to walk when I was one and climb the stairs when I was two. Mom had a field day trying to keep up with me and was livid with my oldest brother for teaching me these things because as soon as he taught me something he returned to college. Mom told me I was a very active infant, never wanted to take naps and always wanting to play. She called the nuns at St. Mary's to see what they did to make me sleep. They told her I was always surrounded by other infants so I must have missed them. Mom was so creative and lined up all of my little stuffed animals around my crib to mimic the babies at St. Mary's and it worked! I would fall asleep more easily and stay asleep. At the age of five, I had eye correction surgery due to a lazy eye. I had my tonsils out when I was six. I remember when Mom came to bring me home—we were at the front door of the St. Joseph's Hospital when Mom warned the nurses that I was going to get sick. They did not believe her and they should have because I did get sick and they had to clean up after me.

I got along with all of my siblings very well and we all had special relationships. Mark, being my godfather, taught me many things about life and was my protector. When I was six and walking home from my friend Kristen Sexton's house, a big bully socked me in the mouth and I cried all the way home. Mark was home at the time and wanted to go and beat up the bully. Mom calmed him down, did not let him leave, and tended to me. I love him so much.

Patsy, who is ten years my senior, was athletic, smart, and seemed to always find trouble even when she wasn't looking for it. She loved taking care of me when I was little, but when she entered high school, she got involved with extracurricular activities, friends, boys, drinking, and drug use. It made for lively conversations at the dinner table of things I did not comprehend, but I knew were not good.

My closest brother in age, Tim, was so much fun to be with. He was smart, funny and artistic. He loved reading and had an extensive library in his room on a shelf above his bed. I remember he would hide my Christmas presents underneath the shelf in a little cubby and, yes I would peek. In the summer time we spent our time at a rented camp, called the Pepto Bismal pink camp. We got up at the crack of dawn to go fishing. We would fill our canteens with orange and grape Crush soda and take our red Adirondack Guide Canoe, first nicknamed the Sting, then the Red Baron, and fished in the dark. We never caught much, but were very happy.

We grew up on Overlook Drive on the west side of Syracuse. After Mark graduated from college, he lived about a mile and a half away in the Hefner Apartment building on Bellevue Avenue. We visited him frequently and I loved being able to see his monkey that lived in his closet. It was not a real monkey—it was a stuffed puppet but was real to me.

Things changed when I turned seven; our life as a family changed drastically. We learned the meaning of true love, acceptance, and fortitude.

Chapter Three
Christmas 1972

It was three days before Christmas and I was riding my tricycle around the house—through the living room, dining room then kitchen and back. There was no time for sledding—too much to do in preparation for our yearly family Christmas party so Mom let me ride around the house. We had forty-plus relatives to cook for which meant a thirty-pound turkey. Tim and Patsy were home doing homework while Dad and Mark were skiing at Toggenburg Ski Slope in Fabius.

The phone call came around four in the afternoon and everyone fell silent. Mark was hurt, really hurt. He fell skiing—caught an edge attempting a jump and broke his neck. He was taken to St. Joseph's Hospital and assessed for the proper course of treatment. The doctors drilled a halo to his skull so his neck was secure and attached him to a Strykker bed frame. A Strykker frame allows paralyzed individuals to be flipped over in bed more easily and frequently, lessening the possibility of getting bedsores. While in intensive care, one doctor noticed that he was fully paralyzed and not breathing and immediately performed a tracheotomy to help him breathe. Mark almost died that day.

I was kept out of the loop. I was too young to see him and all I knew was that Mark was taken away from me. Christmas came and went without much to do. The mood was a solemn one in our home and my family shielded me from the daily hospital news. During morning prayers and the Pledge of Allegiance at St. Ann's, there would be an announcement to pray for my brother daily. My teachers and classmates asked me about him and all I would say was that he was doing better.

After a year or so in the hospital, Mark was released and came to live with us. We cleared out the dining room and made a makeshift bedroom for him. Through his diligent fortitude in occupational and physical therapy he was able to regain the use of his left side and relearned how to walk. It was a miracle that he survived. God must have had plans for him still on Earth. Although he looked and acted differently, I really didn't notice at all. All I knew was that I had my brother back.

Mark was able to return to his apartment after a while and attempted to return to work as a probation officer, but the toll on his body and the stressors of the job were too much for him. Eventually he started providing handicapped children with swimming lessons, which is something he really enjoyed doing. As the years went on, he moved from that apartment to another, and then bought a house, a nice ranch, where he grew elephant ear garlic.

Mark and I talked about many things. We spoke about my schooling, friends, hopes, and dreams. Going out to eat calzones and playing pool at a little bar near his house was always a fun thing to do. He was a great person when he was not drinking. He, like my sister, drank too much and were different human beings when they drank. I knew they were good people, deep inside.

Chapter Four
May 1980

My early years were full of fun and adventure. We were a very blessed family, able to travel to educational places like Williamsburg, Virginia; Sleepy Hollow; and Washington, D.C. I had many friends and enjoyed creating art, and participating in sports. When I was eight or nine, my brother Tim gave me my first box of Faber Pastels. This is when my real love of art started. If you have ever worked with chalk pastels, you would understand that it can be very messy. I made quite a mess while producing incredibly beautiful works of art. Sister Noreen became red in the face and very angry when I used pastels in grammar school at St. Ann's during art class, because I used my fingers to mix colors rather than tissues. She told me I was not using them correctly. I shrugged my shoulders and agreed, but I knew better. I could be as creative as I wanted working with art and no one could put barriers on my imagination.

We went skiing in Vermont during Easter time and traveled to Hilton Head Island in South Carolina in the springtime. We were so fortunate to be able to do all of these incredible things! Sometimes, Mark would go with us to Hilton Head and even though he was a hemiplegic, he did very well keeping up with us. Tim and Patsy also joined us when their jobs permitted them.

Another event that affected me greatly in May, 1980 was when Mom and Dad took Tim to Washington D. C. to look at colleges while Patsy and I stayed home. I was in my sophomore year of high school, and Patsy was asked to keep an eye on me and make sure I went to school and did all of my extracurricular activities. Mark was nearby at his apartment. It was a normal day.

I arrived home from Bishop Ludden High School at my normal time of 3 P.M. watch to *General Hospital*. It was something that I could never do when Mom was home so I took advantage of her absence. Around 4 P.M. there was a knock at the screen door. It was my sister's mental health therapist, two police officers, and an ambulance driver. They wanted to talk to my sister. So I went up to her bedroom and knocked on her door. She often yelled at me and I was used to this abuse, but this time it was different.

She answered angrily and was pissed off that I disturbed her. Her eyes were pitch black and wild looking which truly scared me.

Everyone at the front door followed me upstairs and quickly asked her what she had taken. Now mind you, Patsy had tried to overdose many times and this was just another one of those times. They asked me if I wanted to go to the hospital with Patsy and I said, "Why should I?" and stayed home. I contacted my Aunt Eleanor and she took care of the situation. I did not want to bother my parents or brother with this nonsense and life went on. However, my relationship changed that day with my sister. I'm still working on forgiving, but it is hard to forget how I felt that day.

Patsy was in many hospitals to help her with her issues and they are still a daily struggle for her. Addiction and mental health issues have been a common theme in my family for a long time and it had a direct impact on my choice of career as a Rehabilitation Therapist treating addicts, the mentally ill, and those with limitations. I understand the impact that these issues have on a family as a whole and as well as the addict.

Chapter Five
I Wasn't Hungry

It was summertime in Cazenovia at Mom and Dad's new camp! After renting what looked like a small, doublewide Pepto Bismal camp for thirteen-plus years, my parents decided to buy an older home and barn and remodel them. It was a blessing being on the lake since we swam and enjoyed boating. It was a nice break from reality for a while. We had a lot of parties, bon fires, and stargazing sessions. However, I still felt something was missing. I was sixteen at the time, engaged in art and going out on dates, but still felt very empty inside. I felt that I could not control a darn thing until I discovered something I could control.

So I decided I wasn't hungry one day, then the next and the next. It was freeing and I was finally happy. I ate a little here and there only when people watched in order to hide my anorexia. I started losing weight and looking tired with skin turned whitish-grey. I thought I was fine, but I was not. I started drinking alcohol heavily and that is when I started getting very sick. I started fainting, vomiting, passing blood, and I looked like hell. My father drew a blood sample and took it to the lab for testing and the minute he got home he got a call from the lab. They told him my hemoglobin and Hematocrit (blood counts) were half of what they should be. I could hardly walk or think clearly so he swept me up and took me to hospital and they immediately got an IV started to pump blood and vitamins into me.

After three days of tests, probes, and new ulcer diets, I was finally sent home. My clinical diagnosis was that I had suffered from a peptic ulcer so my secret was still a secret. However, I realized that I almost died and did not want that to happen again. I decided to eat again. I drank heavily and smoked cigarettes. This behavior followed me thoughout high school and college.

High School Graduation 1983

Skiing with Matt at Toggenburg Mountain 1989

Chapter Six
My Roaring Twenties

I studied Ceramics and Art History at Nazareth College. It was pretty easy to get accepted into Nazareth because of my ceramic background. When I was in high school, I was able to take advanced ceramic classes at Syracuse University at night and they were easily transferred to Nazareth. School went well and I graduated in 1987. After I graduated from Nazareth, I lived in Rochester with seven friends while working in an upscale gourmet store.

After two years, I came back to Syracuse and had several retail jobs until I found my calling to work with addicts and the mentally ill. I was able to secure employment at Toomey Residential and worked in a group home for young boys. It was a stepping-stone to other work opportunities. A year after that I was employed at Benjamin Rush, a psychiatric hospital and then Crouse Hospital in the detox unit and in their outpatient facility. I loved my work and was very good at it. No complaints. Wanting to do and learn more about therapy, I decided to go back to school and get my Master's at Syracuse University in Rehabilitation Therapy, Substance Abuse, and Mental Health.

During this time period, I was suffering from a lot of anger and rage. Being away from home allowed me to distance myself from the chaos at my dysfunctional home and my sense of being out of control reared its ugly head again. My brother Tim and mother noticed my issues and suggested that I see a therapist.

Gerda Bothe was my first therapist. Even though she was an MSW, I loved her creative, out of the box way of doing therapy and looking at life. We spoke a lot about self worth and the importance of finding yourself. She eventually changed her name from her married back to her maiden name of Van Dyke. That impressed me greatly. I was twenty-seven at the time and I was able to clean up my act and become more conscious of looking at the big picture and not my tiny world. I remember everything we talked about and it later played a huge role on how I treat clients.

In December1997, I had another bout with death. Being a smoking asthmatic, I had issues with breathing. I was in school full-time and working full-time. To make a long story short, I developed double pneumonia and was hospitalized for a week. I missed Christmas and all the fun festivities. I was so scared the first night in the hospital—they pumped fluids, prednisone, and IV antibiotics into me and I ended up with the classic "moon face" from the steroids. Anxiety was my middle name thanks to the meds and I asked God for help. It may have been a dream or an illusion, but I spoke with little winged cherubs that helped me sleep and ease my mind. It was pretty cool. One thing those little angels and another little one later helped me do, was quit smoking. God had a plan for me.

I finally went back to work at an outpatient clinic in February, 1998 and life was very good. My family was doing well and I got a new position at work after receiving my Master's degree. This is when I met my husband.

Chapter Seven
The Starter Marriage

While I was working at Crouse Hospital's Outpatient Clinic my colleague Judy told me that her boyfriend, Scott, had a friend who was looking for a pen pal. His name was David. Judy was in the Navy Reserves and Scott and David were stationed on a ship in the middle of the Mediterranean Sea. I thought it would be fun chatting with someone so far away and keeping him company. We became fast friends and after six months or so we met in person, fell in love, and decided to get married.

There was one problem; David's divorce was not finalized and his soon to be ex-wife was being stubborn about not signing her paperwork. During this time, I had met David's family who lived in Arizona and we had taken a few side trips here and there. David was now in Norfolk, Virginia and worked at the Naval Operations Base, known as the NOB. He was a sonar technician and when deployed was on a nuclear cruiser. It was exciting for me and I was more excited about the possibility of being in a healthy relationship.

My brother Tim who met and married the love of his life, adopted the first of their three children. Her name is Margaret and she was a catalyst of helping me quit smoking. I took Margaret on walks in her stroller or on my hip and we had so much fun playing silly games. It was springtime and I was ready to take my sweaters to Dewitt Cleaners to make room for my summer wardrobe. When I picked up a sweater, it smelled horrible! It smelled like old, rotten cigarettes and I was holding Margaret the last time I wore it! She was breathing in the carcinogens that I was wearing! It never happened again; I quit smoking April 23, 1998. It was easy and simple, and one of the best decisions I have ever made in my life.

Unfortunately, David's ex-wife died suddenly from an asthma attack. However, her untimely death allowed us to get started on our nuptials. Preparing for the wedding was crazy! Everyone wanted to have a shower for us—we had four in all. The wedding and reception were magical along with our New England honeymoon. The only thing for us to do was to sell my house and move to Virginia. My house sold in nine days and our new home was an apartment in the Pembroke Area of Virginia Beach, Virginia.

After six months of looking for a job, I was employed by the Community Services Board of Newport News, Virginia as a drug court therapist. We moved to Chesapeake, Virginia to a beautiful neighborhood. Our neighbors were great fun to be around and we became fast friends with the couple right across the street from us—Sean and Jody. We went out to dinner, to the theater, and shopped in Norfolk. Many times we traveled to Colonial Williamsburg and hiked at Chesapeake State Park. Holidays were spent at my parents or David's parent's home. Life was good.

In February of 2002 I started developing severe back and leg pain and was given Hydrocodone for pain. It helped the symptoms but never the real cause. David became distant that spring and my father's health started fading. In July, David and I traveled to Italy and were able to be blessed by Pope John Paul II. When we returned home, my father's health got much worse and on July 12th, he passed away. We immediately flew home to attend the calling hours and funeral.

On Friday, August 23rd, a month after we buried my dad, David told me he was having an emotional affair and I knew it was with Jody, our next-door neighbor. I totally lost it. My world fell apart that day. I called my mom and told her what happened and made plans to move home. Since I worked with a drug court, I knew attorneys and judges, so the divorce was simple. I quit my job, moved out, and had the house on the market in a week. My father was definitely helping my every move from the other side. It was a crumbling, crushing time, but I had a feeling it would all work out. It took many years, tears, and finally, acceptance to heal from my divorce. The pangs of loss still affect me today. For instance, I tend to question everyone's motivation for the choices they make that directly and indirectly affect me.

Chapter Eight
Dad's Lazyboy

When I moved back to Syracuse, I decided to live with Mom for a while. Mom and I spent time together in the den: Mom on the davenport and me in Dad's gold leather Lazyboy. We watched the food television stations and chatted about old times. I ate, slept, and lived in that Lazyboy. It just felt comforting. Living with Mom was wonderful; she helped me with loneliness, and I helped her with the new task of living without Dad. We were both dealing with loss, abandonment, and bewilderment. I was beyond depressed and went to my primary doctor, Dr. Cohen, for help. He referred me to Dr. Shapiro, a psychiatrist who not only prescribed medications, but also did talk therapy. Dr. Shapiro also treated my brother Mark so he knew a lot about my family already. It was kismet! I was put on Zoloft and Lexapro for my depression and Elavil and Ambien for sleep. My fatigue and insomnia was through the roof (if that could be at all possible) along with my never-ending back and hip pain. I knew that depression could manifest as pain so I didn't think much of it. Dr. Shapiro also wanted me to see another primary doctor, Dr. Butch.

Mark died six months and a day after my dad died. His nurse found him kneeling next to his bed with his head resting on his bedside table. His bed and night-side table were my Aunt Peggy's and I'm sure were also her mother's, my grandmother's. I have them in my guest bedroom now. I had a dream the morning he died that we were standing in his kitchen chatting. I went to see him and as I was picking on his urinary leg bag, we broke out laughing hysterically. At that moment, my mom knocked on my bedroom door to tell me my brother had died. It made me wonder how much I could take and survive. Well, there is much more to come.

I don't remember much of this time period because things were starting to get a little fuzzy. Mom and I cleaned out Mark's house, and planned the funeral like we did Dad's last year. One thing I do remember was that Mark's funeral spray had three huge cloves of garlic in it, his favorite herb, and something that he grew every year and shared with many.

Chapter Nine
The Calm Before the Storm

In 2003 I was able to obtain a per diem position back at Crouse Hospital doing exactly what I was doing years before. Working on 6 Memorial, the detox unit of Crouse Hospital, allowed me to feel at home again. I worked with the same people I had worked with before and even had my old supervisor. I was able to make pretty good money for working in the social services arena and had excellent health insurance. Along with working at Crouse, I also joined a direct sales company, First Fitness, a wellness company, to help me lose the weight I had gained while on the medications that I had been taking. As usual, I was burning the candle at both ends. I kept myself very busy so I didn't have to think about anything.

Life was going fairly well. I was finally divorced in the fall of 2003, making new friends at both jobs, going out to listen to live music, taking day trips, and enjoying cruises—I had no complaints. I purchased a house and moved from Syracuse to Camillus. The house was purchased in February, 2003, but I did not move in until July since the sellers needed more time to finish building their new house. That was fine because I was still living with Mom. It was about three miles away from her so I could be at her house in a flash if needed.

My new home is on a cul-de-sac and a fun community with great neighbors. I have a pool and a very large lawn that needs a lot of work, but since I love gardening, it was a good project for me. It was July and we were enjoying a beautiful summer. I worked on the garden beds and maintained the balance of proper chemicals in my pool. I hired a lawn crew to take care of my half-acre lawn and trim the trees. Mom used T J's Lawn Services ever since I could remember and the owner,

Tom Gilligan, was and is a good friend of mine and he read my mind as to how I like my lawn. At Dad's calling hours, Tom fell to his knees in front of Mom with his eyes welling up and took her hands into his. It was a touching scene. He was so present and loving then. My parents took the place of his grandparents and he was very close to them. Tom's a good guy and he still takes very good care of me.

While working at Crouse Hospital and fixing up my new house, I also worked at First Fitness. I met wonderful people from all over the country, won many trips, and went to conventions in Dallas and Orlando. I noticed that I was getting fatigued more often, but I just thought it was because I was overdoing it. Other odd symptoms started to pop up. I tripped and fell many times—thinking I was being a bit klutzy. These things were swept under the rug. I remember one time when I was leaving my office, heading to the nurses' station, when my legs collapsed underneath me and I could not get up. I called to Kevin, a nurse whom I knew could pick me up and was nearby to rescue me. He came and asked what I was doing on the floor. I told him I dropped something and we laughed it off. Crazy and scary symptoms were emerging.

From 2004 on, I was a patient at the Syracuse Orthopedic Specialists and Mary Lou Corcoran Physical Therapy facility for my chronic pain and weak muscles. Gold's Gym was my home away from home—I always liked to be active—working out, swimming, and I kept up with it even through my horrific pain. In 2005, my diagnosis was right leg bursitis and this is what my PT treated me for. The steroids and Neurontin helped a little with the pain so I just dealt with the symptoms. Another symptom was insomnia, again, and I was put on Ambien for the second time. It worked for a while.

Mom was having a lot of hip issues and leg pain and on my days off I took her to her appointments and helped her with things around the house. Her age was catching up with her and Tim and I could see that things were getting more difficult for her to do. We all decided that Mom may need full time help at home and we called Medical Registry, a nursing company on West Genesee Street. We had used their services in the past with my brother Mark and my father, and they agreed to take care of Mom. I didn't worry as much about her knowing someone was there. I was able to secure a Certified Nursing Assistant (CNA) through a friend of mine who was a nursing teacher at BOCES. Eventually, Mom had registered nurses during the day and nightnight.

Chapter Ten
Five Element Theory

I decided I wanted to go back to school and study acupuncture at the New York State Chiropractic College in Seneca Falls, New York. Already having a graduate degree allowed me to easily be considered as a candidate for the acupuncture school. The only thing I needed was a science class. I had taken loads of psychology classes, but no science. I ended up taking a 100 level nutrition class at Onondaga Community College. It was a night class and extremely boring. With fatigue setting in more, caffeine became my friend. Coffee saved my life and still does! So I passed the class and was accepted into the acupuncture school.

I love school; I am a nerd, what can I say? The year was 2005 and I was attempting a new career. It would be great to combine it with my therapy background utilizing Auricular Acupuncture on the detox unit since outpatient and drug court settings made me realize how it helps addicts work through many of their issues. I was the oldest student and got along well with everyone. The teachers were devoted and the environment was much different than Syracuse University. My class only had seventeen students in it and the instructors had a very hands-on approach to teaching, meaning that we had sufficient demonstration with our instruction.

Being a commuter, I traveled forty-five minutes to and from school. Living in Central New York, I was used to very snowy winters. Seneca Falls is an extremely rural area and driving there was pretty treacherous, but I did it. Classes were extremely interesting—I always loved learning about the human body and one of my classes was Gross Anatomy. It took me a moment to get used to the smell of the formaldehyde, but I was overwhelmed at what I saw, felt, and experienced. Our Gross Anatomy teacher was Dr. "A" and he was younger than me, in a band, and extremely creative. I remember one class we had was about the cardiovascular system and he started his PowerPoints with a picture of "Vlad the Impaler", better known as Dracula! He asked the class, "Who is this?" No one knew but me! Ha! I was just showing my age.

I took other classes—chemistry, theory, points, herbs, philosophy, Tai Chi, Qi Gong, plus some western medical classes. There was a lot of walking—up and down stairs and running across campus and I was having more problems with ambulating. I was receiving Reiki, a form of energy work at the time, and my Reiki Master gave me a beautiful Shillelagh, an Irish walking stick, to help me with my balance. Oh, I didn't tell you that my balance was being affected and this is when it began. So I used the cane and I felt much more secure during my long trudges across campus, in hallways, and up and down stairs. When I was at school, we could get free acupuncture and chiropractic services, and boy, did I utilize them. My pain was still present and other things seemed to start happening.

Chapter Eleven
Swiss Cheese Brain

Then it came to memorizing the nervous system, the skeletal system, the muscular system, and so on. I learned to make up jingles and songs to keep everything straight in my head. I spent so much time going over how the blood enters the heart through the lungs to the left atrium, left ventricle, right ventricle, and then to the right atrium and to the body. Every time I started the journey, I forgot where I was and had to start over again. Gross Anatomy identification tests consisted of looking through slides and at the flagged body parts in cadavers. My task was to identify what I was looking at, but problems arose when I knew what I was looking at, but for the life of me I could not recall the cell or organ. I felt defeated.

When I was learning acupuncture theory, meridians, points, and especially herbs, my head was even more in a fog. I did the homework, sat in the front during classes, and participated, but was confused all the time. I did very well at writing papers and doing anything creative, but there was so much memorizing—forget it! You need to know I was on the Dean's List when I was attending Syracuse University and graduated with a 3.7 GPA while working full time at the hospital. I could not understand why the brain was not working.

Another one of my favorite classes was Philosophy taught by Anthony Fazio, an acupuncturist who owned Peaceful Spirit in Ithaca, New York. He was kind, patient, and very deep. Along with teaching philosophy, he taught Qi Gong and Tai Qi. Philosophy allowed me to think outside of the box and I did not have to memorize. I could write insightful papers instead of repeating everything I had learned. I understand that learning everything word for word is important in the medical field, but not for this Swiss cheese brain head! I could not do it anymore. When I participated in Tai Qi, I did my best, but trying to follow steps and have my body follow the leader was impossible for me. Ugh! Why couldn't I do any of this? I was a gymnast when I was little, skied for forty-plus years, ran, danced—you name it, I did it! What the hell was happening to me?

I was very depressed and had not seen a psychiatrist in years. The school's insurance plan offered free counseling and I took advantage of it. I had more education than the woman they referred me to and she was very nervous when she spoke with me. Her name escapes me as many names do now. We spoke about class work, teachers, and studies, but never about the "meat" of the matter. At this point, I was working full time in Syracuse, attending school full time in Seneca Falls, and totally confused about my deteriorating brain and body. The therapist asked me one question that I will never forget. "In the worst case scenario, what would happen?" Wow! Where did she learn that line? Well, I would have the answers to the questions, but not for a few years after. As you will soon find out, I soon will be experiencing many "worst case scenarios".

Chapter Twelve
Is There a Doctor in the House?

In order to understand the absolute craziness of my soon-to-be diagnosed illness, we have to go back a few years in order to describe my progression of symptoms. Beginning in 2001, I started seeing an orthopedic doctor in Newport News, Virginia for sudden back and hip pain. Her name is still locked in my void. Her diagnosis was obesity; I had gained weight and had right side bursitis. She prescribed huge amounts of Hydrocodone. It helped a little bit, but the pain never went away. For the next two years I continued to take Hydrocodone and exercised as much as I could, although the pain almost made me vomit. My gut was a mess so I was eating Tums and drinking Maalox continuously.

It was now 2003; I was separated from my husband, my dad died, as did my brother Mark and I lived at home with Mom. My new primary physician, Dr. Carl Butch, was on the staff at Crouse Hospital where I was employed. He was kind and gentle in his approach. The most important thing I liked about him was that he listened to me and appeared to have a vested interest in everything I brought to my appointments. At first I saw him for basic Primary Care Physician issues such as asthma medicine refills, antibiotics when I was ill, or yearly physicals. Very quickly, I was having symptoms of severe plantar fasciitis with the growth of bunions in both big toes. The pain in my feet outweighed the pain in my hips and spine. When hydrocodone was discontinued, I just took aspirin for the pain. You have to understand that my tolerance for the Hydrocodone had increased and it was not working anymore, plus it had ripped my gut and colon apart. Dr. Butch prescribed physical therapy and I went to Mary Lou Corcoran's Physical Therapy in Fayetteville. I saw Matt, a young physical therapist, and he was able to work through the knotted-up fascia in both feet. At this time, I started limping and dragging my right foot because of plantar fasciitis, so I was told. I kept up with my foot exercises of toe raises and arch strengthening.

The pain in my hip and back was getting worse and the aspirin was not cutting it anymore. I had joined Gold's Gym in East Syracuse to stay active and lose weight. Even though I was in constant pain, I knew I had to continue to move. I had always worked out—at Bally's Gym, Champion's Gym, and even Lenda Murray's Gym in Virginia Beach. Lenda was a seven-time Miss Olympia and her husband, Urel, a three-time Mr. Universe. It was a state-of-the-art gym! So I continued working out year round—skied in the winter, and swam in the summer. Dr. Butch thought I should go to an orthopedic physician for my spinal and foot pain.

Since my father had practiced at St. Joseph's Hospital, I chose to go to an orthopedic group affiliated there. Syracuse Orthopedic Specialists (SOS) was very well known and I had experiences with them with broken bones when I was younger. My first orthopedic physical was Dr. Greenky and he referred me to Dr. Glen Axelrod, who specialized in General Orthopedics & Trauma, Sports Medicine, Joint Replacement, and Robotics. When I met with Dr. Axelrod, he diagnosed me with bursitis and asked if I wanted relief from the constant pain. Of course I did! So he explained that I needed to change into a gown and lay on my left side, so I did. He injected Lanocaine in my hip first and then the cortisone. I asked if it was going to hurt and he said, no, it would not. As he proceeded to inject my right side, I thought I was going to die. The pain was absolutely horrible—it felt like someone jabbed a hot knife into my hip. I was bruised and hurt even more. After a few days, I felt better and could move with more ease, but still had a nagging numbness on my right side. I knew that that was not the answer to my problem, so I went back to Dr. Butch to discuss what was next to help with pain and mobility.

I noticed that when I was working out at Gold's Gym, I was having some problems. While riding the recumbent bicycle, my feet kept on slipping off the pedals. Every time I placed my feet back on them, they would slip off again. So I moved over to one of the upright bikes and the fit was much better. My feet stayed on the pedals and all seemed good for the time being. Soon, my gait became noticeably altered; I developed foot drop in booth feet and a progressive limp developed when I walked. I decided to work with a Reiki Master for some relief. A friend Gina Cashier suggested that I see Benjamin, who practiced Reiki and was a metaphysical healer of sorts.

Benjamin lived in Peterboro, about forty-five minutes away from me. I started making treks to Peterboro to receive treatment. When I arrived at Benjamin's house the first time, I found that his lawn and walkway were not handicapped friendly. There was a slight incline in his lawn and I was having a horrible time getting to the front door because of my failing mobility. It almost felt like I was walking on marshmallows.

Benjamin helped me climb up his stairs. His house was adorned with so many plants—I could not count them all. He lives with his girlfriend and they raise chickens in the backyard along with numerous cats, birds, and dogs. His Reiki table was in a little side room with plants and crystals. Sessions lasted around an hour or so and helped with my anxiety, regaining focus and insomnia, but not the ongoing pain and newly developing numbness in my legs and feet. At my fourth visit with Benjamin, he gave me a cane his father made for him and it helped me greatly with walking and stability. I loved Reiki so much that Benjamin trained me and I became a Reiki Master!

I was still attending bi-weekly physical therapy appointments. My focus was working on strengthening my core—sit to stands, ankle and foot exercises, and gait training. I practiced walking frontwards, backwards, and side to side. My walking was not getting better, but I was maintaining. I started scuffing a lot and always had to remember to pick up my feet and toes. To help with pain, my physical therapist applied a TENS (Transcutaneous Electrical Nerve Stimulation) unit with cold and hot packs to my hip and it seemed to help a little. I continued to participate in all that I could—work, family functions, attending conventions, but things kept on getting worse. In 2004, Dr. Butch suggested that I go back to SOS, so I did. Dr. Brett Greenky ordered x-rays and MRIs to identify the problem. It is important to note that I am terribly claustrophobic and every time I had an MRI, valium was ordered for me to take beforehand. He then sent me to my third orthopedic physician, Dr. Stephen Robinson. Dr. Robinson's specialty was neck and back problems.

Now I had one orthopedic doctor to help me with my back issues. I was so happy that they were finally working on a possible diagnosis for all my crazy symptoms. Of course I had more intakes, tests, and questions to answer. "When did you first notice this or that?" "How long had it been going on?" "Any family history?" "What medications are you allergic to?" You know the drill. UGH! All the while, my pain was increasing, walking became more difficult, and I was getting more frustrated. I frequently met with my doctor and his nurse practitioners. At one appointment, I met with a young nurse practitioner to discuss pain relief. She asked me what I had taken in the past and I told her Hydrocodone among other narcotics. She accused me of being drug seeking. I assured her I was not drug seeking, but in horrible pain and she prescribed Tylenol and Lidocaine patches. I found out later I was suffering from neural pain and not muscle or joint pain. Hence, the patches did nothing except leave a stinky, sticky glob of goop on my skin.

The next time I saw Dr. Robinson, he prescribed Ultram, a synthetic narcotic, to help with the neural pain. I was allergic to it. So now it was back to Hydrocodone, physical therapy, strength training, and Neurontin. At this point from 2005 to 2006, new symptoms were popping up. The most annoying one was charley horses in both my calves in the middle of the night that woke me up. I've never suffered from this type of pain—so intense and sudden. I screamed and cried until the muscles released, then finally I could go back to sleep. I had also noticed that the Hydrocodone was not doing a damn thing anymore. I discussed the issue with Kevin, the nurse in detox where I worked, and he said, "Yeah, you still have pain but you don't give a damn about it anymore!" Ha! I agreed. My tolerance for Hydrocodone had increased so rapidly that the amount that I had taken to relieve pain would cause me to become a zombie. It was impossible to work and remain pain free.

The new diagnosis was bulging discs and spinal stenosis. Dr. Robinson referred me to New York Spine and Wellness Center to see Dr. Mary Trusillo who was an Anesthesiologist and certified in pain management. I heard that she was new and my mom had seen a pain doctor in her clinic so I thought it was a good choice. Hopefully, I would be able to manage my pain without heavy narcotics.

It was a very busy office, lots of hustle and bustle—patients with walkers and wheelchairs, filling out multiple forms, and appearing to be in so much pain like me. I filled out the forms handed to me and proceeded to meet with the nurse and later the doctor. The pain clinic received all my x-ray and MRI results plus my office notes from Dr. Butch, Dr. Axelrod, Dr. Greenky, and Dr. Robinson, so she had a good handle on what I needed. She conducted a few neurological tests and then we scheduled the series of three spinal injections that would take place in an outpatient facility near my house. Another thing she mentioned was that she would be prescribing my medications now—specifically my narcotics and that I would be mandated to receive urine drug screens. I understood why; I worked in the addiction field for years. Not a problem. I was prescribed Hydrocodone two to three times a day at 7.5/325 mg to manage pain. It was a pretty hefty dose, but I figured she knew what she was doing.

My first spinal injection was scheduled within a month after we received confirmation from my insurance company. It is important to note that insurance paid everything from the get go: x-rays, MRIs, doctor's visits, narcotics—EVERYTHING— but that too would soon change drastically. I was told that I would be receiving Versed, a type of drug used for anesthesia that heavily relaxes the patient, causes forgetfulness, and for me, seemed to paralyze me so that I would be still during the procedure. With that information, I needed to have a driver transport me because I would be totally out of it after my injection.

I asked three friends to drive me on three different occasions and all said yes. We had to arrive at the outpatient clinic an hour ahead of time for preparation of the procedure which entailed filling out forms, meeting with a nurse, getting an IV started, and making sure vital signs were appropriate. I had excellent veins so getting the IV started was a snap. I received 100 mg of saline solution and when that was completed, the gurney would be wheeled out. It was a chore getting me on the gurney and I needed help from a few nurses, but it was accomplished. The operating room was quite intimidating. It was very cold and as you would imagine, sterile. The nursing team, three in all, had masks, gloves, and scrubs on. My task was to help them transfer myself to the operating table and flip over on my stomach. I have no idea how the hell I did it, but I did. I had a nurse at my head, my feet, and on my right side. The doctor came in dressed as the nurses and explained to me what was going to occur. I was nervous and scared. Prior to the injection, I was given Versed through the IV and everything became a blur. The nurse at my head monitored my vitals and made sure I was breathing and the doctor proceeded with the injection. Since my pain was on my lower right side of my body (hip and leg), the doctor chose to inject my spine between my fourth and fifth lumbar foramen, where the motor and sensory nerves leave the spinal cord and travels to all parts of the body. It is really amazing how they actually conduct this procedure. Since I was semi-conscious, I remembered bits and pieces of the procedure. There is an ongoing x-ray machine that takes numerous pictures of your spine and that is how the doctor knows where to inject the cortisone. When it was over, I was transferred to another gurney and wheeled to the recovery area. After remaining in that area for about an hour or so, I was transferred to a wheelchair, then to my friend's car, then home. The next day, I was sore from the injection and pretty numb from my sacrum down.

This procedure took place two more times and I have to admit I felt better for a week or so after the injections, but that was all. Cortisone is a great drug for many different ailments like asthma and dermatitis, but it beats up on the human body's immune system horribly. For folks with failing immune systems, it can make them even sicker. After a while, the injections weren't doing a damn thing and the Hydrocodone was reaping havoc in my gut so I refused both. The pain clinic kicked me out as a patient, said I was being non-compliant with my pain medicine regiment, and refused to refer me anywhere.

Chapter Thirteen
A New Chapter

In the fall of 2006, Mom was not doing well. She had a few visits to the hospital with possible transient ischemic attacks (TIA) and we could tell that she was failing slowly. Meanwhile, I made the decision to leave school to be closer to home for Mom. At the end of my fifth trimester, I left school, my new friends, teachers, and dreams for a new career. Deep inside, I knew that I might not finish because of my inability to learn the way I used to even though I had tutors and extra time taking tests. It was a moot point. The decision was made and that chapter of my life was over.

Since I was now in Syracuse and not traveling to Seneca Falls three to four times a week, I could spend more time focusing on my issues of depression, loss, and total bodily dysfunction. When I was with Mom or when Mom didn't need me, I would spend more time at the gym, physical therapy, and even at my orthopedic specialist. At this point, my physicians: Dr. Butch (PCP), Dr. Robinson (spinal doctor), Dr. Greenky (hip, knee, foot doctor), Dr. Trusillo (pain doctor), and PT, Mary Lou Corcoran were all treating me for plantar fasciitis, bursitis, bulging discs, and possibly spinal stenosis. Yup, my thoughts exactly—I was really screwed up. Since I was refused care and referrals, I was shit out of luck.

During the summertime, I sought out the help of another mental health therapist, Suzanne, who referred me to another therapist closer to home. His name is Mark Fohs and he has been my therapist to the present day. Mark thinks out of the box. He is a Rehabilitation Therapist like me, has a Neuro

Emotional Technique certification, and also has an extensive background in Chinese Medicine. It was a very good match. We discussed the basic stuff—family history, jobs, education, self-worth—you know the drill. However, he had an interesting way of looking at life. Mark is a tall, thin man and always wears a Jerry Garcia tie that matches his bluish-grey shirt. He has Chinese medicine charts hanging in his office that is painted in a calming, blue hue. Many times when his window is open, we can hear dogs next door at a veterinary hospital barking when they are playing outside. That barking would often distract me from our hour-long chats, but Mark would always reel me back in.

During my counseling sessions, I learned so much about myself and my belief system. It allowed me to develop a really good foundation for what was yet to come. We discussed loss of control, regaining self-worth, and learning about family dynamics. His methods were gentle, yet direct. We worked on congruency in every sense of the word, like how one action would directly affect many others and how these actions imprint every cell in our bodies. We see how the mind, emotions, and body all work synergistically together as we experience life. Yes sir, right up my alley.

Chapter Fourteen
Forty-five Minutes

Anita, my First Fitness pal, and I were in Dallas, Texas eating lunch at BJ's Barbeque Restaurant. Both of us ate like birds and usually shared a sandwich and soup or salad on the side. Today was just like any other day. Halfway into our lunch, I got a call from my brother Tim who had Mom on the line. It was very noisy and I could barely hear her weak, frail voice, but I'm glad we spoke for a short amount of time. Anita and I were in Dallas for a convention and although I knew Mom was sick and in the hospital, she wanted me go on with my life and not worry about her. So I attended my convention.

We enjoyed the convention and all of its festivities of team building, product demonstrations, and of course, the banquet on the last night. Walking was getting more difficult and my friends were noticing and trying to ignore it and so did I. We participated in as much sightseeing as we could and even went to an aquarium during one of our breaks. Everything was a challenge for me. Anita was great to travel with—she was patient, kind, and stuck to my slow pace. I used a wheelchair at the airport because of my increased fatigue and leg pain.

We made our flight itinerary to Pittsburgh, then onto Buffalo, New York. We chose to fly into Buffalo because it was less expensive than to Syracuse. When we arrived, we made our way to the thruway. It usually takes two and a half to three hours to drive from Buffalo to Syracuse. About fifteen minutes into the drive home, I received a frantic call from Tim telling me I had to come to the hospital as soon as I could. Mom was dying. I called all of my prayer warriors and there was a prayer chain put into place. I can't remember who I talked to that day—maybe Debra, Ginny, or Gail—I'm really not sure; it was all a blur. I was sick to my stomach.

We arrived at Upstate University Hospital forty-five minutes after we left Buffalo. I could not tell you how it happened—it could have been a time warp or God, getting us there without incident. However, we were there. Tim met us at the door and carried my bag to Mom's room. She looked so tiny lying on a huge bed. Nurses had placed a bi-pap mask on her mouth that allowed a full stream of oxygen to gently flow into her lungs as she lay in a coma-like state. The death ralls had begun and the end was near. Her heart and pulse were very slow and faded from time to time until she caught her breath. The experience was very scary to witness and lasted for around two hours. When she took her last breath my world stopped revolving. My brother hugged the nurse in the room and I lay across my mother's body. Tim went up to Mother's head and said a few prayers, then the nurse came in to console us while a young doctor came in to declare her time of death. The day was July 12, 2009 at 7:34 at night, the same day my dad died seven years prior, July 12, 2002. I figured they had it planned.

After all was said and done, we drove to my brother's house where I stayed for two weeks and tried to learn how to live without Mom and relearn how to live with loss. That night, I was on my phone, calling friends for support, all the while, crying. I stayed on the top floor of my brother's house and pretty much had the time and space to do what I pleased. I needed to sleep, but could not. All of a sudden, an image of my father appeared—he was dressed in a sports coat and bow tie, wearing his black-rimmed glasses and looking very stern. He told me that it was taking a long time for my mom's progression to the other side so he needed me to go to bed and sleep. He said that he loved me and disappeared. It was amazing and it worked—I fell asleep.

The following days where filled with planning for the wake and funeral, and so on. It all went very smoothly and we used the same funeral hymns and Bible passages as Dad's funeral with one small change. Tim had the congregation sing Mom's grammar school anthem, "Lincoln Shine", during his eulogy and the last song sang was "God Bless America". We received a lot of support from friends, neighbors, and relatives. Everyone was wonderful. Suzanne from

First Fitness was an accomplished opera singer and stepped up to sing with the funeral choir. Now it was back to reality, clearing our mom's house and camp and saying goodbye to many things. I never knew how much help I'd be needing from Mom, Dad, and Mark on the other side of the veil.

Chapter Fifteen
The Aftermath

The next few months were pretty difficult for me, emotionally. I needed something, but I had no idea what I was searching for. My weekly therapy appointments were going well along with trips to the gym, but something was lacking. Tim suggested that I go to a spa in Arizona to help calm my *shen* (a Chinese term meaning spirit), so I researched it and made plans to attend Canyon Ranch in Tucson, Arizona. I flew into Phoenix and had a town car pick me up to take me to the ranch. I actually remember my bungalow number—149; it was beautiful and peaceful. I chose to attend a program at the Life Enhancement Center that focused on healthy eating and healthy mind and soul. The menu for the entire ranch was farm to table, organic and healthy. There was no alcohol or smoking permitted and cell phones and computers were used only behind closed doors. It was a place where you could reconnect with your soul.

Along with healthy eating, I enjoyed working out in the gym, swimming in the three pools, getting Auravedic massages, and receiving metaphysical readings. Canyon Ranch also has a world-class medical facility that utilizes both western and eastern medicine. I took advantage of it all. At this point I was using my cane to get around and frequently I would ask to be transported in a little golf cart due to increased pain.

The following year, I returned to the ranch and had a deeper discussion with one of the metaphysical teachers, named Jonathan, who was the head of the metaphysical department. I had taken all the classes and services they offered, like past life journeys, astrology, numerology, and so on. I tried to do

Qi Gong and Tai Chi, Chinese forms of energy movement exercises, but could not continue because my balance was shot to hell. I really wanted to develop my spirit more so I asked Jonathan what my next step should be. He suggested Nine Gates Mystery School in California. I had never been that far west and it sounded like a good adventure so I took the plunge.

There are things that I am sworn to secrecy about at Nine Gates, but I can tell you Nine Gates made a direct impact on my life and how I looked at the world from then on. I learned things about myself that allowed me to grow as a woman, a daughter, and a child of God. Since my walking ability and proprioception was getting worse, I could not participate in everything the school had to offer, but they made contingencies for me. The teachers and volunteers were inspiring and have remained some of my dearest friends.

One of my favorite teachers at Nine Gates was David who teaches Druidry, a spiritual practice that promotes harmony, connection, and reverence for the natural world. He takes yearly trips to Bali with his students and introduces them to Balinese culture and I took two trips with David's group and loved every minute of it. Getting around was much more difficult than I expected and I needed help with everything I did. This was the last trip I took on my own. I was becoming an invalid.

Chapter Sixteen
Acupuncture, Chiropractic and Physical Therapy – Oh My!

I continued working at Crouse Hospital and tried to live a semi-normal life. I decided to focus on working out more and increasing my physical therapy, tri-weekly acupuncture, and weekly chiropractic appointments to deal with the symptoms that were changing daily. Adaptability became my middle name. My right foot developed a permanent "foot drop" so I was fitted for a plastic leg brace in hopes I would not trip and fall. My chiropractor found no evidence of bulging discs or spinal trauma from the x-rays. *Funny*, I thought then, and quickly ignored it. Gigantic bottles of Wegman's aspirin were at my bedside, kitchen sink, and bathrooms in my house because of my constant migraines.

    I had been getting weekly massages to help with my pain from a massage therapist named David who piped music into the bottom of the massage table while working on my poor, aching body. It was an interesting approach using vibration for healing and I did very well with this treatment. I was not in acupuncture school anymore and had some time on my hands so I started my own therapy practice. I looked for a space to rent. David suggested that I contact a friend of his, Wil, who had a metaphysical practice and had a room to rent. It was 2010 and I decided to rent from Wil whose practice was in Liverpool, not far from my house. I would work per diem at Crouse Hospital and then take care of clients at my office. It was fantastic! We had guest speakers who discussed ancient wonders of the world, palm readers, and healers of all kinds. I was able to incorporate my Reiki training, Auricular Acupuncture skills, and talk therapy with my clients. All the while, I used a cane to get around, gobbled my aspirin, and drank plenty of water. This lasted about a year and a half. However, with increased fatigue, memory loss, and deteriorating mobility, I had to close up shop. I continued to work at the hospital only when I was physically able.

To sum up, I could not work, could not think, was in constant chronic pain, and had no idea what the hell was going on in my life. It felt like my world was coming to a crashing end with nowhere to turn, but to crawl into deep, dark hole to die.

Part Two

Chapter One
A Beacon in the Dark

After working out at Gold's Gym, I went to my bi-weekly acupuncture appointments to have some cupping, a traditional Chinese medicine (TCM) practice that involves placing cups on the skin to create suction and relieve muscle pain. I remember in my Western Clinical class that Lyme disease was being discussed so therefore, I knew something about it. Now mind you, I had numerous Lyme tests done by Dr. Butch, my PCP and all showed negative results for Lyme. Even when I called the Infectious Disease physicians at University Hospital about my symptoms, they told me that Lyme disease did not exist where I lived and I did not have Lyme symptoms. Hum… I was stumped… until today.

When I started my acupuncture appointments in 2012, I hopped up on the table and lay on my stomach and had a Chinese cupping treatment procedure and then needle insertions. Sometimes I would have horrific back spasms for no apparent reasons, or so I thought. After my back treatment, I turned over to have a simple front treatment, starting with the needling of Large Intestine 4, *Hegu*; Stomach 36, *Zusanli*; Spleen 9, *Yinlingquan*; Ren 17, *Dan Zhong*; and an extra point, *Yintang*, my favorite, which is smack dab in the middle of the forehead that benefits the pineal gland and the third eye. My spasms sometimes got so bad I could only place two to three needles per session and so Karen Dellis, my acupuncturist, and I altered treatment plans when the pain and other crazy symptoms emerged.

After a full hour treatment session I asked Karen, "Do you have a protocol for Lyme disease?"

She said, "Why?"

I said, "Well, do you?"

Then she looked at me and said, "Oh my God!"

I said, "Yup, I know, I have Lyme!" Karen had another patient whose son had Lyme and saw a doctor in Virginia. *Holy crap! Virginia? Why don't we have anyone here in Syracuse who knows anything about this illness?* I just didn't get it. So I took the business card that was on the bookstand in Karen's office and worked on conjuring up the nerve the call the name on the card—Dr. Eboni Smith; I was scared shitless.

I was very lucky I was able to secure an appointment in July, in just two months' time. Very quickly, I learned that appointments for specialists take a while to get so it was kismet that I could get one so quickly. For the next two months, I had a tedious task of gathering all of my doctor's notes from all my practitioners and compiling it for my new doctor. My list included one primary doctor, three orthopedic doctors, two neurologists, one pain doctor, one psychiatrist, one mental health therapist, one acupuncturist, two chiropractors, two podiatrists, and two physical therapists.

My head was swirling in a tornado-like haze. Is this what I have been doing for the past ten years? I was exhausted just thinking about my life! What an utter lack of time and energy! All I knew was that I was going to Virginia and would be well again. I was nervous, excited, and ready to heal. It was awesome having someone who would understand what I was going through and not question why I had stopped taking my Lexapro and Elavil.

Chapter Two
The First Day of the Rest of my Life

New Patient Comprehensive Evaluation
It was 4:30 in the morning on Thursday, July 12th in 2012 and I was nervously waiting for the Bellavia taxi to whisk me away to Restin, Virginia from the airport for my very first Lyme disease appointment. The sky was pitch black and there were no cars on the roads so I was able to make it to the Syracuse Hancock International Airport very quickly. I walked with a cane at this point so I needed a wheelchair to get to the plane. It took an hour for Sky Cap to get a wheelchair and after that I checked in and was off to the gate.

In order for me to board the plane, the plane crew had to wheel me downstairs through the airport employee's back corridors and coffee room and then to the tarmac. The airplane was very small, twenty seats in all and it was half full. It took us about an hour and a half to arrive at the Washington Dulles Airport which was ten minutes away from my new doctor's office. The Dulles Airport is huge, to say the least. I waited about twenty-five minutes to exit the plane waiting for the wheelchair, and counted nine elevators that we had to take to get to the curb and hire a taxi. I hired a taxi and made a plan for the driver to come back to my doctor's office when I was ready to return to the airport. The time was 8:30 A.M. and I was an hour and a half early for my appointment. I paid the taxi driver and entered the office building that was next to the Restin Hospital Center. I found a chair right across from the elevators and relaxed until I had the nerve to find Dr. Smith's office.

Dr. Eboni Cornish

While I was sitting and people-watching, I received a phone call from my brother Tim who wanted to give me support for my upcoming appointment. He shared that he had lit candles at Holy Cross Church in memory of Mom and Dad since it was the anniversary of their passing. I had completely forgotten about that—it must have been a sign from heaven that made this appointment possible.

Now I had thirty minutes to get to the Shor Center, to Dr. Smith's office. Dr. Shor was very well known in the Lyme community so it made me very happy to be able to secure an appointment with one of his colleagues. I made my way to the elevator and pushed the button for the second floor and went into room 202. It was a rather small office that seated about five or six patients in the waiting room. As I entered, I was warmly greeted and handed a stack of papers to fill out. All of my paperwork was in a backpack and I eagerly handed it over to the receptionist. I started filling out the pages of medical history, non-existent family history, and present symptomology. It was about five minutes before my appointment and I felt a tap on my shoulder from one of the nurses. She woke me up and caught me in the middle of a snore, and asked, "Would you like to go to a room now?"

I said, "Yes please," feeling very embarrassed as all of my paperwork had fallen on the floor.

After they let me sleep for a bit, I was escorted into a large office where I was introduced to Dr. Eboni Smith, a young, tall, slender doctor who greeted me with open arms. She said that she wanted to know my story so I quickly blurted out what I had been going through the past eleven years and then she told me to stop and take a breath. She told me to take my time and that we had an hour to talk. This was foreign to me. This was nothing that I had ever experienced. A doctor wanted to know about me, my symptoms, and believed me. Weird! She reminded me of my primary doctor a few years ago, Dr. Butch, who listened to me and believe me too. So I took a deep breath and started again, this time much more relaxed and at ease. She wanted to hear everything about my life: my work, education, family, habits—everything. After about forty-five minutes, we went into an examination room where she took my orthostatic vitals, drew blood, monitored my ambulating, and conducted neurological and cognitive tests and guess what—I failed all of them. Dr. Smith could clinically diagnose me with Chronic Fatigue Syndrome, depression, a sleep disorder, plus a possible diagnosis of Lyme Borrelia Complex (LBC). Lyme Borrelia Complex is, in fact, Lyme disease with or without co-infections and multifaceted syndromes. The manifesting symptoms and physical findings that are correlated with Lyme Borrelia Complex are: fatigue, sleep disturbances, non-fibromyalgia, neuropathic symptoms, and mood instability. Now we had to wait on the lab results. Here we go again!

Dr. Smith instructed me on the way they diagnose Lyme disease and how they treat it. She said they follow the International Lyme and Associated Diseases Society's (ILADS) guidelines and treatment protocol instead of the Center for Disease's (CDC) Infectious Disease Society of America's (IDSA) treatment and protocol regiment. I listened to what she had to say, but did not understand *a single word*. What was made clear was that the focus of treatment for me was to put me into remission, not curing me. After further research, I found out that Lyme disease never goes away, much like HIV. It just becomes undetectable. It was also mentioned that there are high possibilities that Lyme symptoms can reemerge from time to time mainly due to autoimmune suppressant medications and trauma. At this time, I was very tired and overwhelmed and really wanted to go home. She wanted to see me again in two weeks, but the only appointment I could get would be next month, August 8th. It was then that I realized that I would be spending a lot of time in airports and on planes, and that I was pretty sick.

I was given several prescriptions, a new diet and meal plan, a strict medication regiment, and a new identity as a chronically ill Lyme patient. Even though I was very relieved about getting a possible diagnosis, I was scared and angry and had too many more emotions to share. So I packed all of my new paperwork in my backpack, paid the $800 bill, and made a call to the taxi service to come and get me for my trip back to the airport. What a day!

The following is my first medication protocol and new lifestyle suggested changes:

- Deplin- 15 mg one tablet daily (methylated form of Folic Acid) to help with brain function of synthesizing neurological chemistry and detoxification of the liver
- Vitamin B-12- 5 mg one tablet twice a day (combined with Deplin for liver detoxification)
- Enhansa- Curcumin (turmeric—reduces swelling and pain)
- Pinella- Nerve Brain Cleanse (absorbs toxins that affect the central nervous symptoms)
- Amantilla (helps with sleep and mood)
- Burbur (absorbs toxins and helps with headache, joint, and muscle

pain)
- Lexapro- 20 mg one tablet a day (monitored by psychiatrist)
- Celebrex- 100 mg one pill two times a day (for pain)
- Proventil &Advair (for asthma)
- Multivitamin
- Probiotic
- Vitamin D3

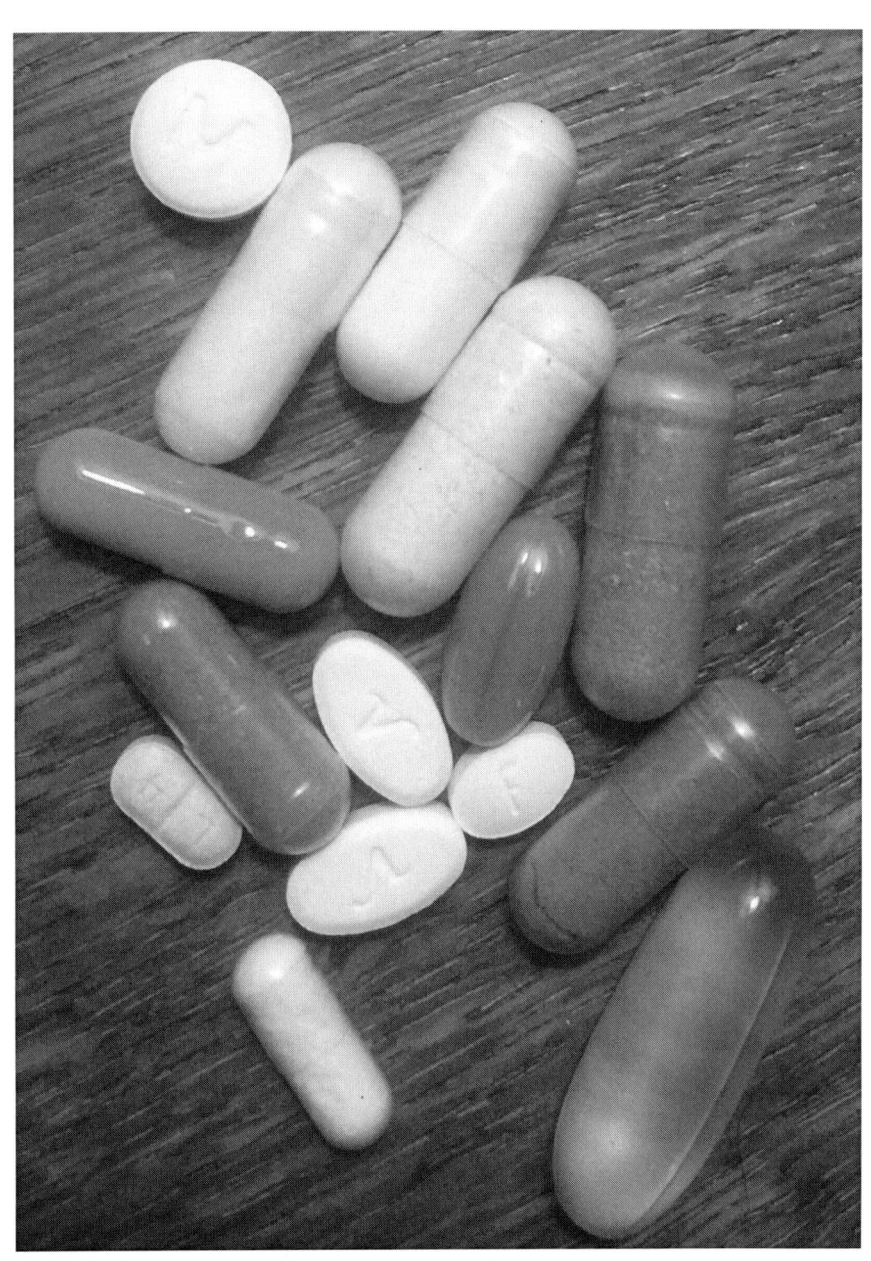

Morning Medications

Chapter Three
Second Visit Initiation of Antibiotics

The time was 4 A.M. and the date was August 8th and I was preparing to head out to the Syracuse airport to fly to Restin, Virginia for my second Lyme disease appointment. I was anxious to find out my test results for my blood screen that was taken two weeks prior. Lab Corp, a testing facility in Syracuse, became the laboratory for all my blood tests and I became very familiar with their procedures and clinicians since I had monthly blood draws. My first blood lab visit consisted of the nurse drawing thirteen vials of blood after twenty-eight orders that were requested by Dr. Smith. I thought I was going to pass out! I was so woozy, but happy that I was able to complete the task.

I arrived at the airport at 4:45 and then to the ticket counter to secure my plane ticket and ask for the Skycap to get a wheelchair for me to get the gate. My flight was at 6:30 so I thought I made it to the airport in plenty of time. I was wrong. It took forty-five minutes to get a wheelchair and then a half hour to get to the gate. At this point, I could stand using canes and hobble through the x-ray machine at security. However, I made it to the gate without a moment to spare because the minute I got to the gate, I had to be whisked off to the plane. Phew! Thankfully, I did it with the help of airline staff!

My flight and trip to the Lyme Clinic was the same as last month, no hiccups. The waiting room was empty upon my early arrival so I chatted with the secretarial staff and read a few articles in the *Field and Steam* magazine. Finally, I was called in to hear my results and to see what the next step would be for me. I told Dr. Smith that my sleep was a little better with the Amantilla and

Turmeric definitely helped my hip pain. My diagnosis remained as Chronic Fatigue Syndrome and depression. Dr. Smith shared that my Thyroid Stimulating Hormone (TSH) and testosterone were very low and could be causing my fatigue.

Most importantly, the test results for Lyme Borrelia Complex were negative across the board for acute, Western Blot IgG, and chronic Western Blot IgM, Lyme disease. It was also negative for all Lyme co-infections: Babesia, Bartonella, Ehrlichia, and Anaplasma. Another test that measures the amount of natural killer cells in the body is called the CD57 test. By measuring the amount of these lymphocytes in the body, it can determine if a chronic disease is present, such as Lyme. The optimum number for a healthy person is 180 and mine was only six. This suggests my natural killer cells were hard at work trying to stop the invasion of the disease in my body and they were losing the fight.

Two more findings that were discussed were my low CD57 and testosterone levels. This correlated with my symptoms with Lyme. Even though my Western Blot tests results were negative through the CDC testing, I knew in my heart of hearts that I had Lyme disease through clinical and physical findings. Upon leaving Dr. Smith's office, I was instructed to make an appointment within six to eight weeks. One new medication Doxycycline, an antibiotic that helps stop the growth of bacteria, was added this visit. It was still a long way home and a long way to recovery.

The following was added:

Doxycycline - 100 mg two pills twice a day MWF

Chapter Four
Third Visit Fatigue, Ataxia, Cerebellar Dysfunction

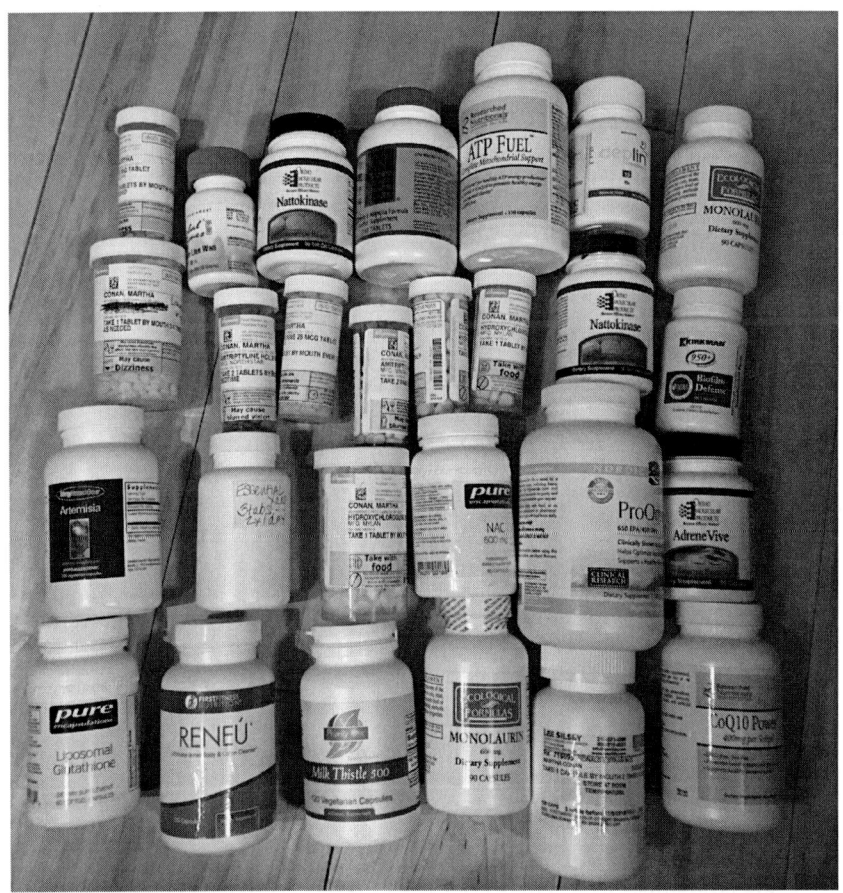

Two months of medication

Today is September 9, 2012 and in just three short months I have already seen my Lyme specialist, three states away, three times! I had to keep on seeing her because she knew what I had, she knew that I was really sick, and most importantly, she believed me. What a nice feeling to be believed and understood.

The third visit started out like any other visit: what has changed, gotten better, gotten worse, and so on. The hot topics this visit were: my sleep pattern seemed better, acute bladder issues due to the Doxycycline, stamina at gym was okay but could no longer do any type of cardio, a decreased appetite, extreme fatigue, ataxia, and increasing neuropathy in my legs. Since I was on a drug holiday (this means a certain period of time being drug free), Dr. Smith wanted to know the results of my "off" week to measure my "breakthrough" symptoms. They were as follows: extreme fatigue, extreme headaches (frontal and occipital), body aches, leg twitches, brain fog, and word aphasia. When I was taking Doxycycline, my symptoms were fatigue and muscle aches and burning and electrical shocks on the bottom of my feet. I learned later that all these crazy symptoms were called "Herxes," better known as the Herxmeyer Effect, which is the result of the body's detoxification processes and it can take many forms depending on what the body is detoxifying from.

As we proceeded with the appointment and my detailed examination, the main issue was a poor gait and ataxia. My depression was not getting any better and Dr. Smith noted that it was possible that it was caused by the Lyme and for me to continue with my psychiatrist. Dr. Smith's next recommendation was to restart the Doxycycline and added two more antibiotics—Cefdinir, another broad spectrum antibiotic that treats many forms of bacteria, and Zithromax, a broad, but shallow spectrum antibiotic that treats uncommon forms of bacteria. I was an antibiotic guinea pig, a much happier guinea pig, but alas, a guinea pig. Looking at my test results from my blood draw on July 13, I was reminded of that one positive Lyme panel—panel 41. Even though I had proof that one panel of the CDC criteria for Lyme was positive, I was not in the eyes of the lords of this infectious disease in the United States.

The following was added:

- Cefdinir – 300mg two pills twice a day MWF
- Zithromax – 600 mg ½ pills twice a day MWF

Six months medication protocol

Chapter Five
Fourth Visit Phone Conference

November 11, 2013 was quite an interesting day. I got up at 3 A.M. and made my way to the airport, just like any other appointment day. Upon arriving at the ticket counter, I asked for a skycap to hire a wheelchair. I waited fifteen minutes, then thirty minutes—no wheelchair and I had forty-five minutes to make to the gate! I asked a second, third, and fourth time for a wheelchair and still no luck. A wheelchair finally came with only ten minutes to hall ass to the gate and guess what—I missed my flight. Thank you United Airlines and Syracuse Hancock Airport! The flight crew told me I could make the next flight, but I would have missed my appointment altogether. I was screaming because I felt absolutely helpless. When they wheeled me back down to the ticket booth to get a refund, everyone asked why I was still in Syracuse. I said because I missed my fucking flight since I could not get to the gate on time. I then demanded the head skycap's phone number and from then on I called him directly when I needed a wheelchair. Being handicapped sucks!

On my way home from the airport, I called up Dr. Smith's office and told them my dilemma. They were very compassionate and allowed me to change my appointment to a conference call. *Excellent*, I thought. It lasted thirty minutes and was much less expensive, around $250.00. I was asked the same questions, how was I feeling, what had changed – good and bad, anything new pop up, and what was helping. In a nutshell, I shared that I felt better on antibiotics than off, my sleep seemed better, I had increased leg twitches and foot burning pain, and increased fatigue mid-afternoon. The fatigue was so bad I had to take a nap every day around two.

To aid in my detoxification, help with herxing, and increase stamina, Dr. Smith added two more supplements: Glutathione and testosterone. Glutathione, simply put, is an antioxidant that is found in the human body that helps with detoxification. Some Lyme patients have lost the capability to manufacture this element due to their compromised immune system and I was one of these patients. Testosterone was to help with energy and, no, I did not grow hair on my chest! So I was given two more meds to add to the list!

Glutathione – 250 mg one pill twice a day

Testosterone and DHEA cream that both work synergistically together to increase stamina and improve adrenal support

Chapter Six
Fifth Visit Severe Herx/Environmental Toxins

Before we go any further, it is very important for you to fully understand that I was always in pain. Always in pain—whether it was muscle spasms, migraines, joint aches, or digestion issues. So to ask me if medications or supplements were helping or hindering my illness, I was at a loss. Image yourself in the middle of the Atlantic Ocean floating on your back and you see huge waves coming towards you and maybe a shark in the distance. This was my life; should I sink, should I swim, what the hell should I do? Well, I keep on paddling to a dolphin, then a manatee, and then to the shore. I have many days like this. You see, as I later found out, Lyme affects your cognitive functions and your limbic system. The many functions of the limbic system involve aiding and monitoring motivation, emotion, learning, and memory. These four constructs were all being affected by Lyme. I told Dr. Smith that I would forget things, many things—forget it—everything!! I got lost when I was driving, could not remember peoples' names, and lost my train of thought in the middle of a conversation. Holy crap! I was losing my fucking mind! My world was crashing down around me and I had no idea what to do. So I looked for a dolphin or a manatee and hung on for dear life.

The date was December 14, 2012 at my next appointment in Virginia, and I was asked the questions of how my new protocols were going. I could not pick heads or tails of anything. "Is the testosterone helping?"

"I don't know."

"How about the Glutathione?"

"I can't recall."

"Turmeric?"

"Maybe."

"Magnesium?"

"Um. I don't know." What can I tell ya, I was brain dead! However, when I was asked about symptoms I totally lit up.

"Are you herxing with the antibiotics?"

"Yes! Yes! Yes! Spasms and pain, pain, pain! Constant electrical shocks in the bottom of my feet all the time, but worse and more in the morning, yes! And yes, sleep was becoming more interrupted with leg and hip spasms."

When my vitals were being taken, I found out that I had gained even more weight and my vitals were abnormal—high blood pressure and fast pulse. Of course they were! I was sick, sick, sick! It was noted that once again I have severe hip, patella, and lower back pain. I had not fallen or hurt myself at all—it was pain from the inside out. Doctors call it idiopathic, from unknown origin. However, I knew better—it was from Lyme and its co-infections. So Dr. Smith added three new items to the list from hell. I was given two prescriptions to reduce my bad cholesterol and lower my vitals, Welchol and Questran powder and one to help combat Lyme, called Lyme Plus. Have you counted them all up yet? Wait—there's more!

The following is my new plan:

Welchol – 625 mg one pill twice a day, one hour from food or supplements

Questran Powder - ¼ scoop daily one hour from food or supplements

Transfer Factor Lyme Plus one gel cap daily first week, then increase to two the following week

Chapter Seven
Sixth Visit Improved Symptoms/Pain

It was a new year and David Patten from Nine Gates Mystery School was planning his yearly trek to Bali and I really wanted to go to get holistic healing for my disease-filled body. I was a little nervous telling my new doctor about my decision to go because of my changing protocols, but I would go to any lengths to heal in some way, shape, or form. I knew that I had to stay out of the sun due to the antibiotic, Doxycycline, which could cause a severe burn. I made up my mind to ask Dr. Smith her thoughts to see if there was another option for something that would not be affected by the sunlight.

On January 17, 2013, I had a fairly good appointment. My symptoms of constipation from the new medications had subsided and my focus and stamina were better too. The Glutathione was really doing a great job with helping me think clearer. I also purchased an infrared sauna to help with detoxification. Infrared saunas are dry saunas that heat up the body quickly while creating an intense detox session. There was a bit of herxing (fatigue, nausea, leg pain) right after, but the next day, I felt great. Chronic pain still remained, but was more manageable.

A few years ago, my cousin Martha became very ill with an invasive cancer and chose to use a Rife Machine to help combat her illness. The Rife Machine was created by Dr. Royal Rife in the 1920's in attempts to alter the frequency of the cells of the human body to create a proper homeostasis. I decided to try a machine called Omdimed, which works like the Rife Machine, to see if it would help me. It did not. Whether it was my illness, the practitioner's experience using it, or the machine itself, it was a horrible experience. I herxed for a complete week after I used it. I realized whether I was on or off antibiotics, it did not make a damn bit of difference. I want to remind you that my primary diagnosis is Chronic Fatigue Syndrome.

It was determined that I needed another antibiotic, Flagyl, commonly referred to as a "cyst buster". Lyme disease is not just Lyme, it is a combination of several diseases and I had several of these diseases. The main bacteria inside of me is Borrelia Burgdorferi and the organism is called a Spirochete, a corkscrew shaped pathogen that can screw itself in every space it wants to in the human body. When it identifies an antibiotic, it cloaks itself as a cyst for protection and multiplies. The way it multiplies is in a very aggressive and intelligent manner. It was time for me to take the plunge and swallow the Flagyl. I had no idea what was going to happen, but I knew that the invaders were multiplying and I had to get rid of them.

Dr. Smith approved my trip to Bali and added Flagyl as well as a supplement, called Smooth and Flow, which helps with constipation. Please see the new protocol below:

- Flagyl - 250 mg tablets one twice a day
- Smooth and Flow - (8 doses) twice a day

Chapter Eight
Seventh Visit Joint Pain/Neuropathy

Daily Medications

When I was in Bali, I was very ill for five days and survived on young coconut water. My friend and our tour guide, Made, brought me a coconut from his backyard every morning. Then, he brought it to a nearby kitchen near my bungalow and drilled a hole in the top and stuck a straw in it. I swallowed the healing nectar and that brought me back to the living. When I was in Bali, I received any type of holistic healing they offered from Reiki, to massage, to traditional healers, and even to Hindu temples to pray with priests. I tried it all!

My medication protocols became very intense and confusing. I took three weeks of antibiotics, one week off, sometimes taking certain antibiotics three times a week, others two times a week. Other medications could be taken together and others could not be taken together. My gut was suffering and I had to take other medications to counteract the constipation, diarrhea, or nausea. I would take medications to sleep and others to wake up. I had to do all this with a Swiss cheese brain. I hated life.

At my seventh appointment with Dr. Smith Flagyl was the cyst buster from hell. During this protocol I had three weeks of Doxycyline, Cefdinir, and Zithromax, and one week off, during that week off I would take Flagyl. When I was taking Flagyl I was bedridden for four days with severe herxing that consisted of muscle spasms, leg cramps, migraines, insomnia, and fatigue. I would double up on magnesium to stop the cramping and Baclofen for the spasms. It was not a pretty picture, especially when it came to bathroom issues.

While I was at my Lyme appointments, I received Myers Cocktail and Glutathione infusions. I wanted to continue these forms of detoxification at home because I was getting wonderful relief from my symptoms. The problem in acquiring IV therapy was getting an infusion company to administer a supplement that was not covered by insurance. Both infusions worked very well with detoxifying my liver and my constitution. It was a moot point because of what I like to call, damn red tape. I contacted all of the infusion companies in Syracuse and the surrounding areas and they had never heard of vitamin therapy or Glutathione and turned me down flat, even if I said I would pay out of pocket. Un-fucking believable!

Once again, a few changes to my protocol occurred. I had a test to see if I had a bio-toxin exposure; Doxycycline was discontinued, so an anti-microbial supplement, Banderol, was added to the list along with me re-starting Neurontin, an anticonvulsant medication. Eight years prior, I was prescribed Neurontin as a sleeping aid and it worked very well, but I was using it for a different reason today, to stop my spasms.

I was instructed to make another appointment in six to eight weeks and get another blood draw that consisted of seventeen orders, mainly to check liver enzymes and different blood and cell counts. My other job was to secure an infusion company and to be as creative as possible.

The following are the latest additions to my medication list:

- Banderol tincture - one drop increasing to twenty, twice a day, except for the last week of the month
- Neurontin capsules – 100 mg one at night, increasing to four if well tolerated

Chapter Nine
Eighth Visit Improved Symptoms/Ataxia

Lots of new things occurred during the past two months. I started using my infrared sauna, participated in a program called Activated Cell Therapy (to try to change my cell chemistry), ordered an ion footbath, and was able to hire a nurse to administer Glutathione Intravenous Therapy. My parents and brother had used a company called Medical Registry to help with their medical issues so I thought I would give them a try. It was a long shot, but it worked. I was able to order all intravenous medications and medical supplies from a company in Louisiana and have a nurse from Medical Registry administer them to me. I received three intravenous Glutathione therapies weekly. I felt extremely ill during these infusions that lasted between one to two hours. Deb was my first nurse and was very kind and patient with me as she inserted the butterfly needle into a small vein near my wrist, and boy did that hurt! In the beginning, it took a while to get a flashback of blood in the infusion tube and she would have to adjust the needle in my vein to secure a steady flow. I got to know Deb pretty well and learned that her seventy-eight-year-old father-in-law was suffering horribly from fatigue and ataxia. I suggested that he have a Lyme test and guess what? He tested positive for Lyme! Yikes!

I was developing heart palpations at night that woke me up and scared the crap out of me. They were so abrupt and uncomfortable they would take my breath away. While I was driving home from the gym one afternoon, I started having palpations again so I called my doctor to see what I should do. The nurse confirmed with Dr. Smith that I should go directly to the emergency room. So I quickly got my butt to Prompt Care to be assessed for heart issues. I arrived at the West Side Prompt Care, provided the pertinent information to the receptionist, waited for my name to be called and all the while my heart was racing. After they called me, I was whisked into a small room and instructed to disrobe from the waist up, put a paper gown on, and wait again for a nurse to see me. When the nurse arrived, he applied the electrocardiogram (EKG), taped connectors to my skin, and proceeded with the testing. He asked me the same questions I had been asked for the past ten years—name, age, history, and so on. When asked why I was there, I told the nurse that I was having heart issues at night and today, they started up in the middle of the day and I was worried. Then, I did the unthinkable—I told him I have Lyme disease and that my symptoms may be caused by my Lyme. Well, that was the wrong thing to say. He immediately got up from his chair, ripped the EKG leads off me, and said they don't have Lyme disease here and I was fine. I learned my lesson that day to be vigilant in keeping my illness a secret if I wanted to be treated fairly.

On April 29, 2014, I had my next appointment with Dr. Smith. I was aware that I did better on antibiotics than off since they were doing a good job at keeping symptoms at bay. Leg twitching had decreased and headaches were less frequent in the past few months. My mental recall was getting better and I was told that my gluten free diet and the absence of sugar in my diet were helping me. The main issue this time around was heart problems at night. I later found out they were a caused by the co-infection, Babesia. Oh joy!

It was determined that I had mold toxicity and hypothyroidism and that I needed Synthroid, but I could not start it due to my heart palpations. Mold toxicity made my body fight harder to detox and hypothyroidism caused me to have a very low body temperature, pulse, blood pressure, and respiration. I was always cold, tired, and moody. Another test was ordered to measure my Melanocyte Stimulating Hormone (MSH), an anti-inflammatory, regulatory hormone made in the hypothalamus.

This visit I received a Myers Cocktail infusion along with a Glutathione infusion. We discussed possibly stopping Flagyl and Zithromax, and added Welchol for biotoxicity and Samento, an antimicrobial supplement. Samento's dose was a little tricky—take one dropper, twice daily, except for the first three days of the months for three months. The following was added:

Samento - one dropper, twice daily, except for the first three days of the months for three month

Chapter Ten
Ninth Visit Detoxification/Increased Fatigue

Today, we chatted about the importance of a proper diet, the use of footbaths, detoxifying baths, infrared saunas, oxygen therapy, and gut health. The only thing I was not aware of was oxygen therapy. It's called Hyperbaric Oxygen Therapy. It is a pretty interesting concept. The way it was explained to me was that one of the bacteria that I have in my body that causes Lyme is called a spirochete and survives in an environment containing very little oxygen. If it is exposed to large amounts of oxygen it dies. The way it is administered is in a large, sealed chamber, much like a huge iron lung that helped polio patients. The cost is exorbitant—$385 a pop! That was out of the question! A good idea, but not for me—not covered by insurance—you know the drill. I was discovering that nothing was covered by my insurance company and I did not understand why.

I knew that I had to take the antibiotics to kill the bacteria that resulted in an overabundance of toxins caused the herxes. I then had to combat the herxes with proper detox methods. It was a never-ending cycle of total confusion. Try doing this with a clear head, then try doing it with a head just trying to stay afloat—semi-impossible. The herxes this time consisted of insomnia, muscle spasms, pain in my legs and feet, fatigue, anger, and rage. I also began to consistently get lost while driving. I would forget where I was going! I was told that was normal for Lyme patients. Really? I was only forty-eight years old!

My low vital signs were becoming more of a concern so Dr. Smith decided to prescribe Synthroid, a medicine to help my thyroid gland that manages these bodily processes. She said it would also help with my chronic fatigue. I agreed once more to take another medication. You see, I would do anything to feel better. This doctor knew what I had, she was treating it, and it was making a difference. I was being heard, not dismissed, and treated for the correct illness!

A few friends believed that I was sick, while others just dropped off the face of the earth. Some family members kept on telling me I was going to be okay and not to worry. A few of them even questioned my diagnosis and mental health. Yup, some people really suck. I learned that this illness leaves you alone and frustrated most of the time. There was an acronym we use in Alanon called HALT, meaning hungry, angry, lonely, and tired. When these issues come together, it is time to sit down and assess what the heck is going on in your life to make you feel this way. I have to HALT a lot because Lyme had affected how my brain processes information of all kinds. I learned that I had to look inward and not let the outside world affect me so much. Chaos or trauma of any kind in my life also causes the herxes. Life is tough and once I got the hang of just surviving, it became a little easier to live.

So we added Synthroid to the mix and I was anxious to see if and how it would affect me.

Synthroid tablet - 025 mg ½ daily and advance to one if tolerated

Chapter Eleven
Tenth Visit Conference call

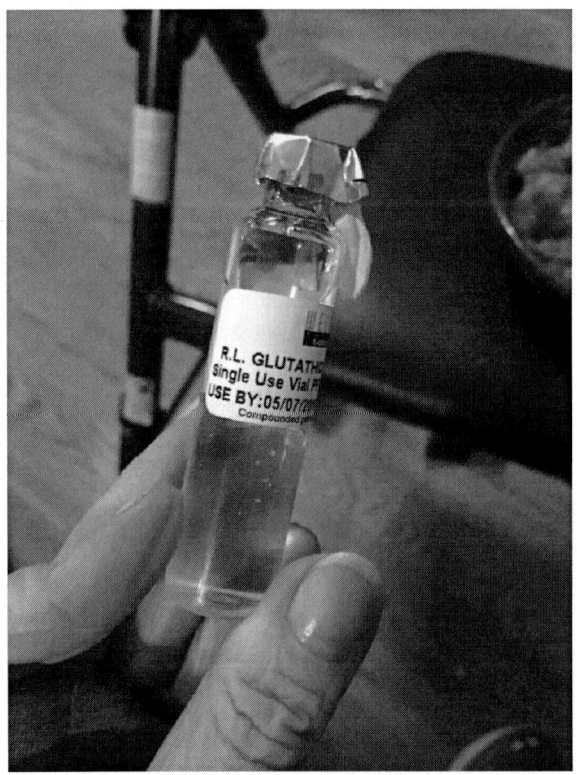

Vial of Gluthathione

During this conference call, on September 19th, I had mustered up the courage to ask Dr. Smith if I could receive IV antibiotics. I was still receiving IV Glutathione at home and felt I could handle it. Over the past few months, I had researched different Lyme protocols specifically to treat neural Lyme because I wanted more aggressive treatment. The common drug of choice used was Rocephin and it had a good outcome for folks like me. So I shared my concern and thoughts on the matter with Dr. Smith. I asked if I could sit down with her, and her colleague, to get his view too.

We discussed my medications—what was working and what was not and my main complaints. The Synthroid definitely helped with my fatigue, sleep, and stamina and even though the antibiotics made me herx, I knew I needed them to kill the infection. All the chelation medications, like Zeolite and activated charcoal, definitely reduced the severity and consistency of migraines. I shared that I really wanted to get off all the sleep medications. She said we would work on that.

My main concern was my depression. I was not walking or moving better. Pain was a daily nemesis and I was following everything to a T—what I ate, drank, and how much I slept. I went to the gym three days a week and I did not drink alcohol or eat sugar. Life was a waste of time for me. Being Catholic taught me to look at God for help. I was sick and tired of looking at God for help because he was not helping me. Maybe He was, but I was not experiencing any help at all. My hate for God would rear its ugly head from time to time. Why He would allow His children to suffer so much, I had no fucking clue. We weren't on very good terms for a while.

I guess I struck a chord because Dr. Smith put me on a brand new antibiotic protocol! I was being heard! Yes! We worked on sleep, detoxification, and antibiotic hell. I was to use the infrared sauna three times a week at 130-140 degrees for a half hour, take another sleeping medicine, Elavil, and add three new antibiotics: Cipro, Mycobutin, and Cefdinir.

- Elavil – tablet 10mg at night
- Cipro - 500 mg tablets twice a day on Monday, Wednesday, and Friday
- Mycobutin - 150 mg capsules twice a day on Monday, Wednesday, and Friday
- Cefdinir - 300 mg capsules twice a day on Monday, Wednesday, and Friday

Chapter Twelve
Eleventh Visit Conference Call

The benefit of being on antibiotics is simple: I'm killing the damn bugs inside me. The problems that arise from being on them are side effects ranging from diarrhea, constipation, rashes, nausea, migraines, fatigue, and so on. Along with taking antibiotics I had to remember to take the probiotics, eat a clean diet, and drink tons of water. The bacteria in my body is brilliant because it can learn to adapt and recognize what I was ingesting and killing it, therefore I would need to alter my strategy and tactics to identify the enemy and destroy it. This is why I had to use as many forms of antibiotics to address the Lyme and co-infections still left. It is a very tricky game to play. I felt like a lab rat and looking back at it today, I was amazed at how much crap I would put in my body to try to get back to normal. It was blind faith. At this stage of the game, no one really knew how to treat what I had, yet they never hesitated to help me. That made me feel very happy and I knew I was in the right place at the right time. The date was November 14th, almost two months since the last call.

Not many integrative medicine physicians treat Lyme disease but are willing to look outside of the box in developing treatment plans and protocols. When I treated my patients, I did the same thing, meaning I would study the whole person: their behavior, strengths, weaknesses, and challenges. Dr. Smith and her colleague, Dr. Shor, did the same thing. I was not a cut-out-cookie, I was a real person with several problems that they were treating. Although Dr. Smith asked the same questions every time I met with her, the questions were fact-finding clues to see what had changed, what remained the same, and what was needed for me to improve. I understood the concepts of treatment, but definitely not the disease, not yet.

My herxing was pretty violent this time around—fatigue, spasms, insomnia, migraines, poor appetite, and a systemic rash immediately following the Cipro ingestion. My IV nurse, Mary Kay Gillis, commented on it first and actually saw it spreading from my chest downward. She recommended Benadryl for the itching and in case I developed issues with my breathing. That did the trick. I immediately contacted Dr. Smith's office and after speaking with the doctors, I was told to discontinue that medication. I was a little upset because when I took both Cefdiner and Cipro together, my foot pain diminished, but I can't take something I am allergic to.

We looked over all my blood tests that were taken this month and the results were still the same: thyroid low, testosterone low, vitamin D low, Glutathione low—I was still a mess. My list of medications, ranging from herbs and vitamins, antidepressants, sedative hypnotics, endocrine supplements, analgesics, muscle relaxants, and anti-epileptics still grew longer and longer.

This time around I was going to start another cyst buster combination, Lactoferrin, a multifunctional protein and its counterpart, Xylitol, an alcohol-sugar sweetener. This protocol was taken on Mondays, Wednesdays, and Fridays, but not with iron supplements or antibiotics. The way it works is that I would take the Xylitol and Lactoferrin that work synergistically to entice the bacteria to come out of their cloaking device, called biofilm, and gobble up the sugar. An hour after that I would follow up with the antibiotics, Mycobutin and Cefdinir, to kill the freed bacteria. Utilizing this protocol, I would also have to be very vigilant with detoxification with activated charcoal, drink a lot of spring water, and increase oral Glutathione, IV Gluathione and take Curcumin, a form of Tumerin. Herxing with be intense, but had to occur, that is why detoxification is so important.

Additions to my medication list:

- Enzaline – digestive enzyme, take with large meals, once a day

- Lactoferrin
- Xylitol
- Activated Charcoal – 280 mg, 4 pills twice a day
- Curcumin – 600 mg twice a day
- Syallgen – environmental allergies powder, sublingual, three times a day with meals

Chapter Thirteen
Twelfth Visit Sleep/Digestion

December 19th was a very frigid day and once again I had to travel to Restin, Virginia to meet with Dr. Smith. It was about 4:30 in the morning and pitch black outside when I climbed into my car to go to the airport. This time I made it to Virginia without a hitch. I knew that I was having some issues that needed attention and consequently, it was going to be a rough appointment.

Holidays were becoming very difficult for me to deal with ever since I got sick. Healthy people have difficulty with the hustle and bustle of Thanksgiving, Christmas, and New Year's. Imagine shopping for presents, decorating a house, attending parties, getting dressed up, and having to act cheerful with chronic pain. I shot death rays out to anyone and anything that got in my way. Yup, that is what the holidays are like for me. My sensitivities of light, sound, and smell are so intense that I become nauseous and aggravated at the drop of a hat. I also have to focus on not eating sugar and gluten, or drinking alcohol. I did my best. A year ago on December 24th, I was rear ended by a drunk driver at a stoplight. My car was in the shop for a month and a half and I had a few bumps and bruises. So I had a hard time appreciating this time of the year.

It really didn't matter if it was warm or cold out, I always hurt. Now I was having problems sleeping, with my gut health, and appetite. We discussed what I should be eating at the parties I might be attending. My focus was on increased probiotics and digestive enzymes to help with my digestion and this affected my appetite. It was suggested that my poor appetite and desire to eat was caused by the amount and types of medications I was ingesting, along with the multitude of bacteria that were floating around in my body. Oh joy! Dr. Smith used the term "early satiety", which meant that I felt full only after a few bites of food. In other words, I had very poor digestion. Ugh!

We also discussed ongoing pain and tremors. Dr. Smith was concerned about past trauma I might have endured. My stamina at the gym was decreasing and it was really difficult for me to do any type of cardio exercise. These were all markers for deeper issues, so I was told. She wanted me to have imaging of my spine done to see what might have occurred. I told her I have a long record of MRI images that she could take a look at and that MS and ALS had already been ruled out as a cause for any ongoing problems.

There were a lot of medication changes this time. The following medications were discontinued: Baclofen, Celebrex, Lactoferrin, Xylitol, Mycobutin, Cefdinir, Banderol, Samento, and Curcumin. In one week I should resume Curcumin, Banderol, and Samento. She also wanted me to incorporate Theralacto to help with digestion along with the other digestive supplements.

New medication additions:

- Celebrex - 200 mg one tablet twice a day
- Curcumin – 150 mg one tablet, increase to two capsules twice a day
- Neurontin - 400 mg at night, increase if needed
- Naltrexone - 1.5 mg three tablet nightly, at refill increase 4.5 mg one tablet nightly

Chapter Fourteen
Thirteenth Visit Improvement of Symptoms/Neuropathy

At my next appointment, February 27, 2014, some of my symptoms seemed to be getting better mainly due to medication changes, however, new ones were erupting. I kept on going one step forward and three steps back—I just could not win. The pain in my hips and back was better along with the digestion issues. Although the Glutathione tri-weekly infusions were difficult to get through, along with the Myers Cocktail infusions in the office, the outcome always benefited me.

The Herxheimer reactions, although infrequent, were intense and brutal. They caused me to cry uncontrollably, scream, yell, curse, and cause self-harm, and made me look haggard. I think this is why so many Lyme patients are diagnosed with mental issues. It's an ugly and scary scene to watch, even if you know it is a symptom of the disease. Once, I was so angry I could not lift my leg in my car, that I punched my car door so hard I thought I broke my hand. Yup, it's that bad sometimes.

This month, the heart palpations came back in full force along with teeth grinding at night. It took me an hour or so to fall asleep and then to be woken up two to three times at night, gasping for air and holding my chest. My body would be sore from head to toe, especially my jaw from the teeth grinding. The fatigue during the day had diminished, but I was still hanging on by a thread. At night, I took Ambien, Amitriptyline, Naltrexone, and a few other herbs to help with anxiety and tremors. Sometimes I wanted to put a gun to my head!

Last month, I had a DNA analysis to identify the presence of mutilated genes. At this appointment, I received the results that revealed I had two major mutations in this specific subset of genes that help rid the body of toxins. I just shrugged my shoulders and said, "Next! What else can happen to me?" This happens to a lot of chronically ill patients so I was not alone. Guess what? The remedy was another pill! Methylated B12, a vitamin, also known as folic acid. So it was added to the endless list and it was supposed to help with many things, especially gut health.

Dr. Smith was going to take a new approach to treating me that involved more meditations and supplements. She added Mora, and reintroduced Cumanda, Samento, and Banderol. These herbs are all antimicrobials that treat Lyme and Babesia. Since Babesia was causing all of nighttime issues along with my hypothermia issues, Dr. Smith also added Lumbrokinase, an African herb made from earthworms. It is an enzyme that helps break down the fibrin in the biofilm of the bacteria. Yes, it has the potential to cause herxing. It was believed that I had a biotoxin illness that was a direct result of the Lyme invading my body. This causes a chronic systemic inflammatory response. This is why I was in so much pain and it is so important for me to focus on detoxification twenty-four seven. The amount of Celebrex I was taking was decreased and soon I would be weaned off of it. I was realizing that I was not really getting better, I was just getting to the core issues of this disease. Life is a constant struggle, but I am strong and will get through it.

The following are new additions to my list from hell:

- Lumbrokinase - two tablets daily before meals
- Celebrex – 100 mg one to two tablets as needed
- Mora - twenty drops, twice a day
- Cumanda - twenty drops, twice a day
- Banderol - twenty drops, twice a day
- Samento - twenty drops, twice a day

Chapter Fifteen
Fourteenth Visit Mood Instability/MTHFR

This appointment, on April 24th, was a very difficult one. Remember when I said, two steps forward and three steps back? Well, this time it was five thousand steps back. This was not due to any medication protocol, diet restrictions, or sleeping issues. It was what this disease was doing to me and how my body and mind were processing everything that was going on in, on, and all around me. I could not walk the way I used to. I could not think the way I used to. I lost friends and family because they thought I was full of crap or wrong about my illness, and most importantly, I lost my faith in God.

Toxins were in every crevice of my body. They caused my migraines, brain fog, and even poor appetite. My sleep seemed better, but my Lyme rage, anger, and self-pity were abundant. I could not control my feelings. Every day Lyme rage caused me to scream at the top of my lungs, usually when I was alone, but sometimes not. My therapist said much of my pain was due to emotional upset—this I knew, but could not control it.

I was still on Lexapro, but Dr. Smith added Field of Flowers, an herbal emotional remedy tincture. The best time of the day for me was when I was at the gym. Lifting heavy weights and doing a thousand sit-ups at a time allowed me to release so much pent up anxiety and made me actually feel that I had accomplished something. There was one problem. Nothing could touch my depression, but I was a master at covering every emotion up ever since I was little, so I just dealt with it.

The mold toxicity issues and the two MTHFR (Methylenetetrahydrofolate Reductase) gene mutations were causing a lot of problems with my mood, dietary, and pain problems. However, nothing was changing with my ambulation. At this time I used two ski poles to walk and keep my balance. I had been sitting for so long that I could hardly stand up straight or keep my head up. My spasticity in my legs had also increased so magnesium was added to help relax my muscles. Many Lyme patients who suffer from similar neural issues use IV antibiotics so I wanted to also. I asked time and time again, but because I lived in another state it was not recommended.

Dr. Smith added another round of Lactoferrin and Xylitol and a chelation protocol. She also suggested Berberine, an herb to help promote a healthy immune response. Compromising biofilms were also be added. N-Actylcysteine (NAC), and Vitamin B12 injections were given at the office to help with detoxification and Glutathione production. I was really getting sick of all the medication and herbal additions and changes, but blindly followed her lead because she is after all, a doctor who treats Lyme.

The following medications were added:

- Field of Flowers - twenty drops, twice a day
- Vitamin B12 - 1000 mg once a month
- Deplin - 15 mg capsules once a day
- Fish Oil - 2126mg once a day
- NAC - 600mg one capsules once a day, increase to two capsules

Chapter Sixteen
Fifteenth Visit Phone/Conference

July 12, 2014, it has been two years to the day that I had met Dr. Smith, and things were not better, they were worse. Yes, I could sleep a little better and had more energy, but that was about it. I took three medications to sleep and several to keep me awake. I could not poop on my own and some days I could not leave the bathroom because of diarrhea. When it came to peeing, I either could not go or could not hold it. I know what you're thinking, it all related to my gut health, but I was taking so much for clearing my gut. My medication and supplement list was getting longer and I was so confused. I would do *anything* to get well. During the past two years, I had tri-weekly infusions that made me ill, flew to Virginia from Central New York every other month for appointments, and swallowed abundant amounts of pills—too many to count! It is important to note that before I was diagnosed I was not able to swallow pills. Today, I can swallow fish oil pills the size of horse pills without skipping a beat. My life had changed so much!

This treatment was getting old, very old, and my bank account was dwindling. It was suggested that I apply for disability, but I refused because I knew I was going to get better and did not want to ask for governmental help. I started going to International Lyme and Associated Disorders (ILADS) conventions and really enjoyed listening to the knowledgeable speakers and learn more about the illness. I even met Dana, one of the women in the award winning documentary, *Under Our Skin*, who suffered from Lyme disease. She was so kind and caring. It was a very good experience and it gave me hope.

Dr. Smith and I also revisited my numerous MRIs this visit and the results were still negative. It astounded me that my previous doctors thought that I had either MS or ALS. Why didn't they have the fortitude to look outside of the box and search for answers instead of keeping me in a box that seemed to fit symptoms they saw? I was growing more and more angry. I needed help and would do anything to get it.

The plan of Lyme attack this month was to focus on detoxification, gut, bowel, and brain health. Of course more supplements were added and there were more protocols to learn—like I said, blind faith. I took more medications and supplements to poop, not to poop, to sleep, stay awake, ease my gut, clean my liver, clean my kidneys, clear my brain, stop my spasms, stop the pain, take a breath, and stop heart palpitations. Enough was enough!! I was so sick of this crazy shit.

My new supplements added this time around:

- Teasel Root – sublingual one drop, three times a day
- Coconut Oil – one to two tablespoons, daily for oil pulling (a technique to absorb bacteria in the mouth by placing coconut oil in the mouth and swishing it around and spitting it out)
- Mapalo – one to two drops, neurological support twice a day
- Mediclear Plus – one scoop in eight ounce glass of water
- Magnesium Malate – two capsules twice a day
- True Fiber – one to three scoops a day
- Vitamin B12 – once a week

Chapter Seventeen
Sixteenth Visit Improved Sx/Dysbiosis

Now I was diagnosed with Dysbiosis. It is the medical term for an imbalance in or on the body caused by an unhealthy change in the environment of the body, especially the gut and mucus membranes. When the body is affected by this condition, it negatively affects how the body fights invading pathogens. I could not take it anymore. It never ends. Like I had I mentioned, two steps forward, three steps back. When it appears to be getting better, it would never last for long. I would have spent an evening out with friends and have a great time, but the next two days be stuck in bed. No matter what I did, no matter how hard I tried, nothing mattered. My therapist became very concerned about my mood and my sessions increased to every week. Depression was my middle name and hope was at a standstill. I was tired of trying and considered giving up.

August 8th was the last appointment I had with the now Dr. Cornish, formerly known as Dr. Smith. She was recently married. The clinical questions she asked were the same as usual: "How did you sleep?" "Any pain in your feet?" and so on. We discussed detoxification and information about diet and new supplements. I was so fucking sick of this crap because nothing was working or seemed to be working. My neurological symptoms of twitching and spasms had increased and were affecting my eyes, ears, heart, and legs. Even though I wanted to die every day and there was no foreseeable end to the hell I was living in, I kept on going and kept on trying.

When you look at me seated, I look healthy and content. When I try to stand and walk, you see my pain. When I was leaving a handicapped parking spot at Wegman's grocery store, I was stopped by a police officer who asked me why I was parked in a handicapped spot. I pulled out my red temporary handicapped tag and told him I have Lyme disease and can't walk well. He did not believe me and asked me why I took the tag down from my rearview mirror. I told him it was because at the bottom of the car tag there are instructions to only hang it when parked. I didn't get a ticket, but it still hurt. At times, I wish that all the people who didn't believe me about being sick would get bitten by a tick and experience what I go through every day. Then, I say, no, I would not want anyone to go through this pain. I don't wish this on anyone.

The last medications prescribed by Dr. Cornish:
Houttuynia - twenty drops for Lyme and Bartonella
Krill Oil Natrol - 1000 mg one tablet, twice a day
Magnesium Malate

Final Medication List
- Activated Charcoal
- Amantilla
- Ambien
- Berberine
- Burbur
- Celebrex – 100 mg
- Celebrex – 200 mg
- Coconut Oil
- Cumanda
- Curcumin
- Deplin
- DHEH
- Elavil
- Florastor Caps
- Field of Flowers
- Glutathione - 1,200 in one oocc normal saline
- Houttuyna
- Krill Oil Natrol

- Lexapro
- Magnesium Malate
- Mapulo Neural Support
- Mega Fish Oil
- Mora
- N-Acetyl-L-Cysteine
- Neurontin
- Normal Saline - 100 cc bag
- Peripheral - IV 24 gage Anthiocath and tubing IV placement
- Pinella Brain Cleanse
- Provent HFA AERS
- Relax Tone
- Serrapeptase
- Synthroid
- Syringe - 27 Gage
- Teasel Root
- Theralac
- Thorne Research Mediclear PLUS
- Vitamin B-12
- Vitamin D - 50,000 IU
- Vitamin D3
- Zavita

Part Three

Jennifer Goldstock, ANP-BC & Dr. Ronald Stram

Chapter One
A New Plan, Stan

Enough is enough! What the hell was I doing to my body? I understand doctors don't know everything, but come on, forty-plus medications, endless supplements, and intravenous supplies, and I still feel and look like crap! Something needs to be done to allow the medical community to treat Lyme disease correctly. After watching the documentary, *Under our Skin* and the television show, *Monsters Inside Me* where Lyme is identified and treated, the question is why are individuals suffering so much and why is it so hard to believe when we tell our doctors that something else is wrong with us. I felt so discounted when I was having heart palpitations and the nurse told me to leave after I told him I had Lyme. It reminded me of the time when I asked for help at Upstate Hospital and they told me that no Lyme existed in Syracuse. The wind was slowly leaving my sails. My bank account was being drained because my health insurance did not cover something that had no positive result even though I had clinical proof.

Attending the Lyme support groups really helped me a lot; I realized I was not alone—we were all very sick. I met individuals from all over Central New York and was able see the struggles they had were very similar to mine. We connected on a very deep level while chatting about our issues and small accomplishments. It is hard to have a support group with sick people, but it can be done. After giving it a lot of thought, I decided to take the plunge again and look for another Lyme doctor closer to home. After contacting five Lyme doctors in New York, the only available Lyme clinic was two and half hours away in Delmar, New York, a tiny suburb of Albany. I thought it would take months to secure an appointment, but much to my surprise there was a cancellation on September 14th! It was kismet and I was in! Due to my fatigue and pain, I asked my nurse, Mary Kay, to ride with me for my first appointment and take notes because of my poor memory. So the date was set and I was ready to start all over again. Prior to my appointment, I rifled through all of my old doctor's notes, medication lists, and pill bottles to present to my new doctor. I was nervous, scared, and ready to heal.

When I told members of my family and friends that I had a new Lyme specialist, some of them were very supportive with pain in their eyes and others were skeptical. One cousin, who is a nurse, reamed me out for being so stupid, that my parents would not be proud of me and I was an idiot for not going to New York City and John Hopkins for treatment. She said I probably had a tumor in my spine. She shared this after a nice meal in her home in front of two of my friends while we were on a trip to Vermont, one of my favorite places in the world. She went on yelling and screaming for twenty minutes while I was sobbing and falling apart, and then she said that I would end up in a wheelchair. HA! Little did she know, I was already using one. She is my Godmother. Well, she was not godly to me. I have since forgiven her, but will never forget. Some people kept on saying that I had MS and to stop making everything up. Soon, I realized that this is what it is like being sick. There will always be people who didn't believe and that was going to have to be okay. I was very much alone except for a handful of people.

Chapter Two
Here We Go Again

Mary Kay picked me up at my house at nine in the morning on September 14th for my 11:30 appointment with Dr. Ronald Stram, an ILADS trained physician in Delmar. He owns The Stram Center, an integrative facility that treats Lyme and cancer patients. In preparation for my frequent visits to the center, I purchased an EZ-Pass for the New York State Thruway. As I hobbled to Mary Kay's car, I placed the EZ-Pass tag on the dashboard and we were off to Delmar! As usual, I was nervous, scared, and hopeful that this time things would work out and that I would be better. While traveling we discussed many things—IV protocols, medication lists, and my hopes and dreams for recovery.

Delmar was so easy to get to and right off the thruway so we arrived right on time. I remembered how early I would have to get up to get to the airport to fly to Virginia, pray that I make my flight, hire a taxi to get to the doctor's office, and then turn around and fly back home. Man, it would take a whole day and keep me in bed the following day. This time it would be different; I would be in one state and possibly get insurance to pay for everything—something—anything! As we followed my phone's GPS from the thruway to Kensington Avenue, we arrived at a tiny, little yellow house. Was this it? Was this The Stram Center? Holy crap! What did I get myself into? It looked more like a country doctor's office. Oh well, we were here and decided to head in. We parked in the back of the house in a small parking lot and made our way to the front door. Then, I noticed there were four steps I had to climb. I had a cane, but the stairs were a struggle to get up and with Mary Kay's help I was able to climb them.

When I entered the office, I told the receptionist who I was and she escorted me to the tiny waiting room. Amy, Dr. Stram's nurse, came into the waiting room and brought me to Dr. Stram's office. She was a young, tattooed clad, pretty woman. I felt very comfortable with her. Then Dr. Stram entered the room. He was small in stature, but had an immense presence. He did not wear the conventional white jacket, just slacks and a nice button down shirt with a stethoscope wrapped around his neck. Mary Kay sat to my left and he sat in front of us without a desk between us. He spoke with a soft, gentle voice and asked me what I needed. I was shocked to be asked that question. Maybe it was a joke or he was testing me; I was not sure. I still really didn't trust doctors. It was about 11:45 in the morning and I was dead tired. So I thought about the question and answered with, "I want IV Rocephen and a PICC line. I never met any Lyme patient with neurological difficulties like me who did not have IV antibiotics."

Dr. Stram said, "Okay, let's see what we can do." Holy crap, he actually listened to me, or maybe that was something he always said. He took blood and my vital signs and asked a few questions.

Since I took an appointment that was a cancellation, it was a fairly short appointment so my full assessment would take place the following month. What I did appreciate was that he was going to revamp my entire medication list. Yes! Yes! Yes! What was going to happen this time around? Would I be able to think without forgetting things, remember words, stop stuttering, regain my hearing, walk normally, stop heart palpitations, harness the migraines, and so on? It was all a crapshoot. I was ready to start again.

New medication list:

- Plaquenil – 200 mg for Lyme
- Minocycline – 100 mg for Lyme
- Rifampin – 300 mg for co-infections
- Milk Thistle – two capsules for Gastrointestinal Issues
- Vitamin D - 50,000 mg once a week for immune system
- Gluathione for my Methylation pathway

- NAC - one capsule, twice a day for Methylation pathway
- Artemesia herbal support
- CoQ10 – 400 mg for inflammation
- Serrapeptase for inflammation
- Curcumin for inflammation
- Deplin – 15 mg for fatigue
- Banderol
- Seamento
- Teasel Root
- Levothyroxine – 25 mg
- Lexapro
- Celebrex
- Fish Oil
- New additions to start on October sixteenth:
- Probiotic
- Nattokinase
- Vitamin D3 liquid

```
IGENEX IGM RESULT            NEGATIVE
CDC/NYS RESULT               NEGATIVE
            18 kDa.      -
         **23-25 kDa.    -
            28 kDa.      -
            30 kDa.      -
          **31 kDa.      IND
          **34 kDa.      -
          **39 kDa.      IND
          **41 kDa.      IND
            45 kDa.      -
            58 kDa.      -
            66 kDa.      -
         **83-93 kDa.    IND
```

Igenex Laboratory CDC results showing 4 panels indication Borrelia burgdorferi, Lyme bacteria, present but not enough for the CDC to present with a positive result, 2014

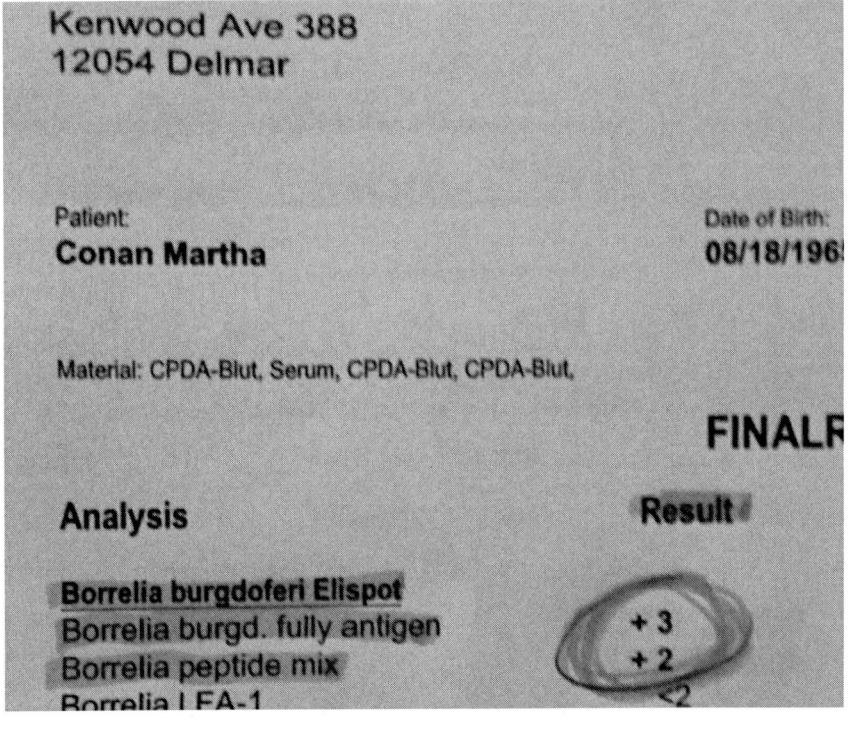

Positive Lyme results from ArminLabs, Augsburg, Germany via the Stram Center, 2014

Chapter Three
Positive

My dad, who was a physician, told me to address doctors as Doctor and so I called him Dr. Stram when he asked me to call him Ron. Along with all clinical testing Dr. Stram had done, he also drew my blood and sent it all the way to a laboratory in Germany for more sensitive testing, and today was the day I was to receive my blood results. The test contained the results for a complete blood count that included red blood cells, white blood cells, inflammation reports, vitamin levels, and also acute and chronic Lyme disease levels. The chronic was just as important as the acute because it helps to determine how long I have had the infection. This time, my friend Cathi Dutch came with me for the long ride to Delmar. Cathi's son, Ben, has Lyme too and has gone to my previous clinic in Virginia for treatment so Cathi was well versed in proper Lyme disease treatment.

I did not meet with Dr. Stram this time, but with Jennifer Mager, a nurse practitioner. It was all the same to me—doctor, – nurse, I really didn't care, I just wanted to get well. If I remember correctly, this appointment lasted two to three hours and was very intense. I had a head to toe physical and answered so many questions that my head spun. The pivotal point of these three hours occurred about thirty minutes into the appointment when I received my test results. Guess what? They were positive across the board for acute and chronic Lyme disease! I went wild—screaming and crying, uttering horrible things about every person, doctor, nurse, anyone who did not believe that I was sick. I was happy, sad, frustrated, and ready to kill the bastards inside of me. Now insurance would pay for my treatment, medications, and everything that I needed to get well. (Little did I know Blue Cross Blue Shield covered very little, if anything at all.) However, now I could get a PICC line approved and get well. The use of a PICC line would deliver IV antibiotics directly into my heart and bypass my digestive system. It would also have the ability to break through the blood-brain barrier killing the bacteria in my brain and spinal cord.

I was able to receive more diagnoses: joint arm pain, joint leg pain, pain joint involving multiple sites (including migrating pain), malaise, fatigue, and spinal stenosis of unspecified region. These would also definitely help my insurance claims. Another herb was added to my protocol called TBB Plus that was an antimicrobial German supplement that did similar things that Doxycycline did in searching and in eradicating the Lyme bacteria. It also had quite a punch when it came to toxicity overload after the bacteria die-off causing continuous herxing. However, when I herx, I knew I was doing something right. Jen, my nurse, started the paperwork for securing my PICC line and also a new IV office protocol for Zithromax and Glutathione. Soon I would be traveling to Delmar three times a week for my new IV antibiotics. Dr. Stram actually did what he was going to do! We started on the tri-weekly IVs until my insurance approved me for the PICC. All was good and I finally had a bright outlook on my future.

Additional medication:

- TPP Plus - herbal detoxification medicine

Chapter Four
The New Beginning of my Personal Hell

It's hard to believe that it took over fifteen educated practitioners and over ten years to figure out that I had bacteria in my body that caused me to want to blow my head off every day because of the pain, frustration, anger, resentment, and self-loathing. *Totally unacceptable*! If I was a wealthy celebrity I might have had a fighting chance of being believed. However, even so, these folks suffer just like I do. I praise the brave who come forward and even though they are not believed, have their personal lives thrown into the spotlight and their reputations ruined for the possibility of living life Lyme-free. Cheers to you! Oh, to have a chance to go to Germany and have stem cell therapy, hyperbaric therapy, or even intravenous ozone therapy! What an intangible concept for the average Joe like me! Well, back to reality.

The time has finally come for IV antibiotic therapy with Zithromax. It is similar to the Z-Pack that some take when they have an infection, but more intense. Dr. Stram chose this antibiotic instead of Rocephin, the one more commonly used because I believe that I had already been on Cephdinir, a form of Rocephin. Luckily, my insurance approved me for IV therapy that included the antibiotic, all medical supplies, and home nursing because I would be self-administering my doses through a Peripheral Inserted Central Catheter (PICC) line. Another choice was a central venous access devise, better known as a port. As I understood it, a PICC line would be a better fit for me because of the easier insertion and maintenance. That explanation will come a little later.

My focus now was driving to Albany from Syracuse in the middle of December to receive my triweekly antibiotic and Glutathione infusions. The dates of my infusions were Wednesday, December 17; Friday, December 19; Monday, December 22; and Tuesday, December 23. I was instructed to have a driver with me because, most likely, I would be sicker than a dog after the treatments. Funny word, *treatment*, one would think it would be healing. Well, it was most definitely NOT!

I arrived at The Stram Center at 11 in the morning and Bridget was my nurse. She is a tiny little thing with auburn hair who wears retro-shaped eyeglasses. Greeting us with a smile, she asked if my companion, Mary Kay, my forever nurse from home, would like to join us and ushered her to a small chair next to me. I offered her an encouraging look, and she said yes, and took out her iPad to do some work. Let me describe the infusion room. Picture this: a tiny room with two recliner-like chairs that had matching side tables for medical instruments, drinks and other necessities. There were empty IV poles, cups with ice chips, and the kindest, most loving nurses that you could ever imagine. I was scared shitless once again! This was my time to heal and to get back to what I had lost ages ago! I was ready. With tears in my eyes, I sat in my designated chair and listened attentively to my instructions.

Bridget told to me to relax and take a deep breath while she prepared the infusion bag of saline solution and Zithromax. After the antibiotic infusion, I was also going to get a Glutathione push, which was a small amount of Glutathione delivered through the IV tubing to help with liver detoxification of the antibiotics. Bridget put on her sterile latex gloves and swabbed my left antecubital site for my very first antibiotic infusion. I was used to IVs; Mary Kay was a pro at finding my veins, and so was Bridget. Bam! She was in and we saw a flash back of blood. She screwed on the IV tubing and started my drip. I immediately felt sick to my stomach and had to lay back and put my feet up. Fifteen minutes into the infusion I had a cold pack placed on my forehead and sucked on ice chips. In another ten minutes, I was administered Zofran, a drug used to prevent nausea and vomiting. To say the least, I was not a happy camper. The infusion took two hours because Bridget had to run the drip so slowly. After the antibiotics were administered, I received the Glutathione that helped me process the Zithromax through my body more efficiently. I slept all the way home. The next three infusions played out the same exact way, but were much more manageable because I knew what to expect. This was going to be my journey for a while now and I accepted it. Now it was time to get my PICC.

New Medication:

- IV Zithromax - 500 mg

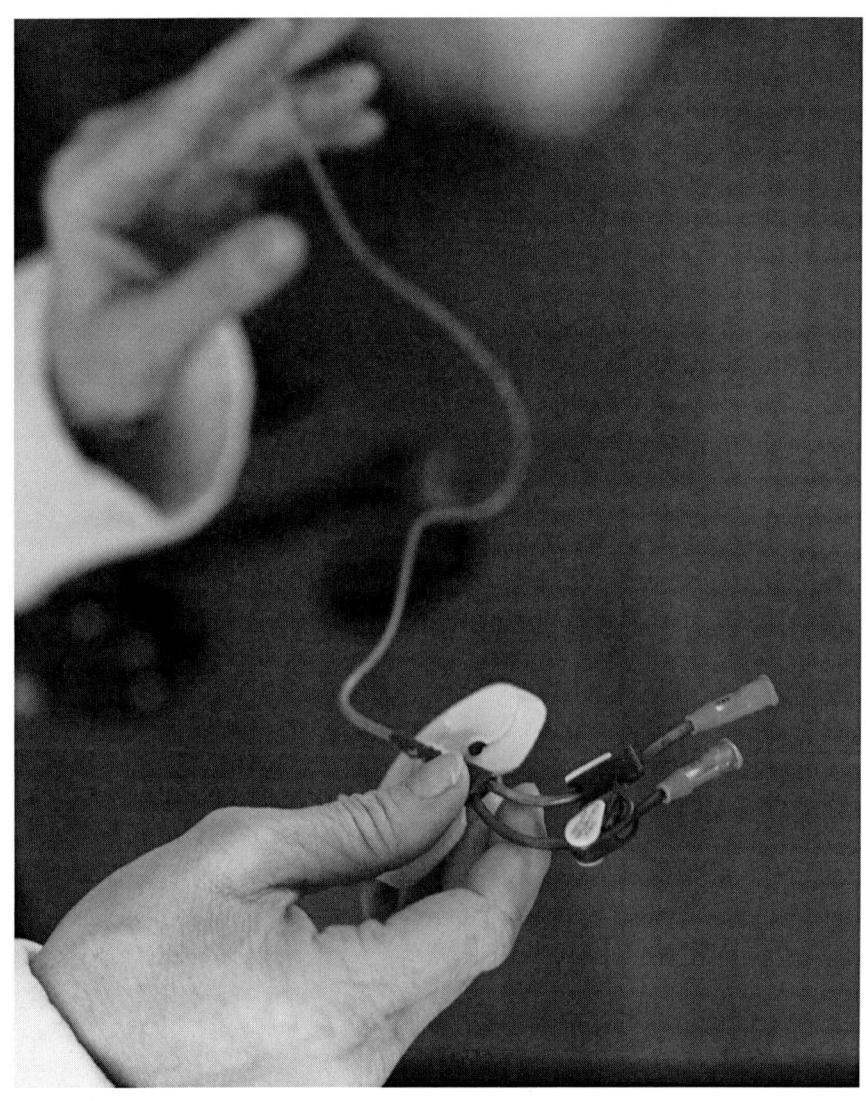

PICC Line

Chapter Five
Merry Christmas!

Dr. Stram received word that I was scheduled for PICC line placement on December 26th! What a wonderful Christmas present! YEAH! I could not wait! Once again, May Kay accompanied me to Crouse Hospital for my PICC line insertion. In preparation for this type of surgery, I read as much as I could from my medical textbooks to videos online of what would take place. They used similar methods for the spinal injections, but I would be awake and coherent the entire time. I was ready.

Upon arrival at the hospital, Mary Kay and I were escorted to the radiology department and then to a pre-operational space. I still walked with a cane so one of the attendants was kind enough to find a wheelchair for me so we could make it to my scheduled appointment on time. Matt was my surgical nurse and he instructed me to undress and put on a gown. He then proceeded with the intake questions that consisted of my name, address, and why I was there to receive a PICC line. The first few questions were easy to answer. However, he wanted to know who sent me to get the PICC and what condition I had to cause me to receive IV therapy. I was scared and did not know what to say, thinking he was going to refuse to treat me like every other had. As I looked at him with my eyes tearing up he said, "You go to The Stram Center, we have lots of patients from there."

I was so relieved! I said, "YES I DO! I have Lyme disease! Will I still get a PICC placement? Please?"

Matt said, "Calm down, we treat a lot of Lyme patients."

I was transferred from my bed to a gurney and then to the operating room. It was white, cold, sterile, and scary. There were three nurses and one was Matt. I was glad to pick him out under the scrubs and surgical mask. A nurse practitioner came in and she was the one who was going to insert the line. I was once again transferred to a very narrow operating table, lay supine with my left arm stretched perpendicular to my body and taped down securely. Everyone wore plastic eye shields, including, myself, along with masks. This was serious shit! In front of me on a screen I could see an incredible image of a continuous series of chest x-rays with a beating heart and arteries and veins—holy crap, it was mine! The nurses dowsed my arm with Betadine and I felt a few small needle pricks and the Lidocaine was administered. I was instructed to turn my head away from the injection site to lessen the possibility of infection. Then, I felt a slight tugging on my arm, looked up, and saw a black line on the monitor in front of me heading towards my heart. I learned that this was the PICC line and it deposited itself in my supra venacava—this was the main vein that goes into my heart. WOW! I was tearing up again and Matt asked me why I was crying and I told him I was happy. He didn't understand, but I did and that was all that mattered. The process took no more that fifteen minutes and I was ready to go home and start my treatments.

After the Lidocaine wore off, my arm was extremely sore. I had a triangular shaped PICC line sterile dressing that consisted of a line that went directly into my arm and had two lines coming out. One line was for medication and the other for flushing. I was taught to wrap up the PICC and to protect my arm. There was so much to learn, but that would come in time. I would be meeting with my infusion nurse the next day and she would show me the ropes of PICC line maintenance.

Chapter Six
Zen and the Art of PICC Line Maintenance

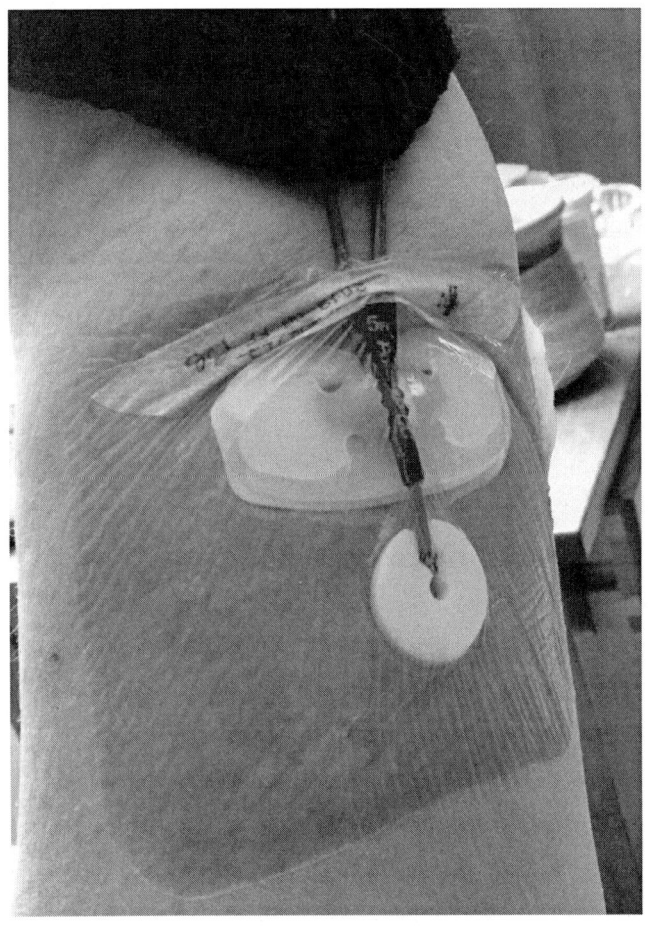

Left Arm PICC placement

It took about a month for the small hole in my left arm to stop hurting from constant rubbing of the thin purple plastic tube entering my body carrying medications that I hoped would cure me. Some patients who had a PICC line administered actually had it stitched to their arm. Luckily, that did not happen to me. It was December 27th and I had my first appointment with Bridget, my new Coram infusion nurse. She was a young mother with two sons who had been in the infusion field for around three years. Bridget shared with me that she took care of many patients with similar issues as mine and this made me feel very comfortable. Prior to this appointment, three boxes of medical supplies were delivered to my front door, one of which was on ice and needed immediate refrigeration. When Bridget saw the unopened boxes, she immediately opened them and arranged the supplies in an orderly manner. The first was an IV pole. When Mary Kay and Deb infused me with Glutathione, we became very creative hanging my IV bag from anything we could clip it to in order to allow gravity to kick in and get the fluid running into my arm. IV poles make life much easier to administer medications.

We then went over the basics of PICC line maintenance. The first was that I needed to keep my arm wrapped up all the time so that I would not catch it on anything and pull it out of its placement in my heart. The next was learning the concept of the acronym SASH, meaning Saline, Antibiotic, Saline, and Heparin. This meant that when I administer my antibiotic, I must first push a tube of saline, then the antibiotic, then saline once again, and finally Heparin. There were bags of white tubes full of saline and yellow tubes of Heparin. The antibiotics were in little, tiny bottles in the refrigerator along with the saline solution. The antibiotic would be drawn out of the bottles and added to the bags of saline, and warmed up, of course, before attaching it to the long tube that was destined for my PICC. We discussed universal precautions, and my antibiotic protocol of Monday, Wednesday, and Friday administrations. Bridget would be coming every Monday morning to change my dressing and check for infection.

My family room looked like a hospital room with plastic gloves, Purell hand sanitizer, gauze, alcohol pads, surgical tape, red plastic bottle needle receptacles, and an IV pole. Over the next few months, it became old hat to me. My procedure for antibiotic administering went this way:

- Remove antibiotic from refrigerator, apply Purell, put on sterile gloves, secure the dull needle to syringe, and draw out the fluid and inject it into the saline solution bag.
- Wait fifteen minutes for it to warm up.
- Unwrap my PICC line tubes, take off the purple end caps of the tubes, and swab them with an alcohol swab.
- Push a tube of saline solution.
- Hang the antibiotic bag and attach its tube.
- After the antibiotic was administered, push saline then Heparin. Heparin avoids clots and it is mandatory in the PICC line.

In the beginning, the entire process took around two hours because the Zithromax would make me feel so ill with nausea, dizziness, and pain that I had to slow down the IV to slow drip. One time, my heart raced so fast that Bridget almost had to call an ambulance, but instead she administered several pushes of saline and I was able to relax and calm my heart down.

On days when I did not have antibiotics administered, I still had to maintain the line with saline and Heparin. It was something that I had to adapt to and it was a pain in the ass, but very necessary. When showering, I wrapped it in a long plastic sleeve that was tightly adhered to my arm. There was a valve on it and I was able to pump air out of the sleeve so it was skin-tight. It had to be clean and dry at all times.

Sleeping with a PICC was another journey. One night the wrap came off and I dislodged the line and as you would expect, I had to have it replaced. Prior to getting it replaced, I wanted to get a hold of my doctor who was unavailable. Instead, I contacted Dr. Daniel Cameron, the president of ILADS who had come to Syracuse to speak at a few events to promote Lyme disease awareness. He kindly answered my questions and assured me that I was going to be fine. The next day, I was able to secure an order for PICC line replacement. It was pretty interesting how they do it. I went to Crouse Hospital once again and had the same nurse practitioner as I had before placing my PICC. As I was laying on the cold gurney, she once again took my arm and placed it perpendicular to my body. By the use of the x-ray imaging, she guided a wire along my present PICC. She then removed my old PICC and replaced it with a new one. When I left the hospital, the nurses gave me a new PICC line card that I placed in my wallet and carried with me at all times. I had completely forgotten that I was originally given a card. This card contains PICC line type and length. This time I would be more aware of what I need to do in case problems come up.

I was able to add Glutathione pushes after my infusions to help with liver detoxification. So instead of a simple SASH, it was saline, antibiotic, saline, Glutathione, saline, and finally Heparin. I was actually able to go on a cruise to Panama with my PICC. Luckily, I was on a medication holiday so all I had to do was flush my line daily and have dressing changes every week which was quite a challenge on a moving ship. I got approval from the ship's physicians, but had to bring directions for them to follow because they had no idea about PICC maintenance. The nurses on the ship wanted to buy my Glutathione pushes because they used Glutathione for healthier skin. I declined; my liver detox was too important.

This crazy PICC schedule lasted for a little over a year. The wrapped tubes were so cumbersome when it came to walking with my cane, walker, and eventually, wheelchair. I would have monthly blood draws (finally pain free) and the ability to receive other medications administered at The Stram Center a little more efficiently. I did not do much during this year due to my PICC, but tried not to isolate myself so much. More information will be discussed about my journey with this purple tube in my arm as this story continues...

Chapter Seven
Phone Consultation

Receiving Infusions

On February 10, 2015, I had a Lyme disease follow up. Due to the snow-covered road on the New York State Thruway, it was best that I stay home and have a phone consultation to go over my new protocols and how I was adjusting to my new appendage. It started out like any other appointment: going over my present medication list, assessing issues that were arising from the PICC line, addressing the amount of herxing I had been experiencing, and fielding questions that I had been journaling during the past few months. The diagnoses that were added this time around were malaise and fatigue, unspecified arthropathy site pain, and influenza (I had a cold). Same old story—I was tired and always in pain. UGH! We also discussed the upcoming cruise I was going on and received information for the physicians on the ship to adhere to. It was great that I was able to do what I wanted, but I was going to do what I wanted anyway. I was so sick and tired of being sick!

Jen was very happy with my adaptation to the PICC line and with my fortitude to do everything I could to get better. Much like Dr. Cornish and Dr. Stram, she gave me strength to forge ahead. She shared that she would be adding more antibiotics to the mix in order to combat the enemy in my body from all sides. I knew what this meant. I was going to get really sick once again. That was fine. I was up for a good battle. When I ran my therapy groups at the hospital, I would never let my patients say they felt fine. They would ask me why. I responded, "It is because the word FINE means fucked up, insecure, neurotic, and emotional." HA! Yup, that was me! So I just went with it! She added three more heavy-duty oral antibiotics: Rifampin, Minocycline and Plaquenil. They treat malaria, cat scratch fever and anaplasmosis—all different types of bacterium, but had to be killed differently. To make a long story short, I was on four types of antibiotics that were *kicking my ass*. I had to be very mindful of my probiotics and gluten, sugar, and dairy-free protocols.

My weight was slowly decreasing because I had no appetite. My gut felt like it was on fire the majority of the time, but that was over-shadowed by my chronic migraines and neuropathy. I was a real mess, but I continued to go to the gym and walk around the track and lift a few weights from time to time. Folks who I saw at Gold's Gym on a regular basis knew when to talk to me and when to leave me alone because they recognized my decreased stamina.

Thank God I continued with as much movement as possible because I would not be alive today if I didn't.

New medications that were added today:

- Rifampin – 300 mg one cap daily
- Minocycline – 100 mg one cap twice a day
- Plaquenil – 200 mg one cap twice a day

Chapter Eight
Phone Consultation Lyme Disease Follow Up

Now Lyme appointments took place monthly if possible or at least every other month due to my IV therapy. I was still sick, very sick. When a Lyme patient takes as many antibiotics as I do, there is an overload of toxins being dumped into the body that can manifest in a number of ways. This appointment addressed many of those issues.

This time, I was too sick to make it to Albany so we spoke on the phone. I had been bedridden for the past five days with sweats, sneezing, coughing, full body pain, and fatigue. Since my goal was to get off Lexapro, an antidepressant medication, I had cut my ingested milligrams to half the recommended dosage and this created emotional distress to arise. I had lost control of everything in my life and this was a small step to regain a little control in my life, as small as it was.

The questions were the same as Dr. Cornish's:

"Do you feel better or worse?"

"Better, I guess."

"What are your most prominent symptoms?"

"Left foot and hip pain, brain fog, constant muscle spasms, and fatigue.

"What symptoms changed?"

"Sleep, I guess, memory, I guess."

"Any gastrointestinal pain?"

"No."

"Any yeast symptoms?"

"No." It was a broken record. The most debilitating symptom for me at this point in time was brain fog. It makes me feel like an Alzheimer patient—forgetting words, getting lost driving and forgetting who or what I was just talking about. It was so debilitating.

Jen, my nurse practitioner, had more diagnoses and consequently, other issues to address this time: spasms of muscles, generalized anxiety disorder, depressive disorder, malaise, and fatigue. Thank God no new medications or protocols were added this time around and I scheduled my next follow up in five weeks. I was preparing for an upcoming cruise to Central America and would be on a medication holiday for two weeks so we decided to see how being off antibiotics would affect me.

Chapter Nine
Cruising to Panama

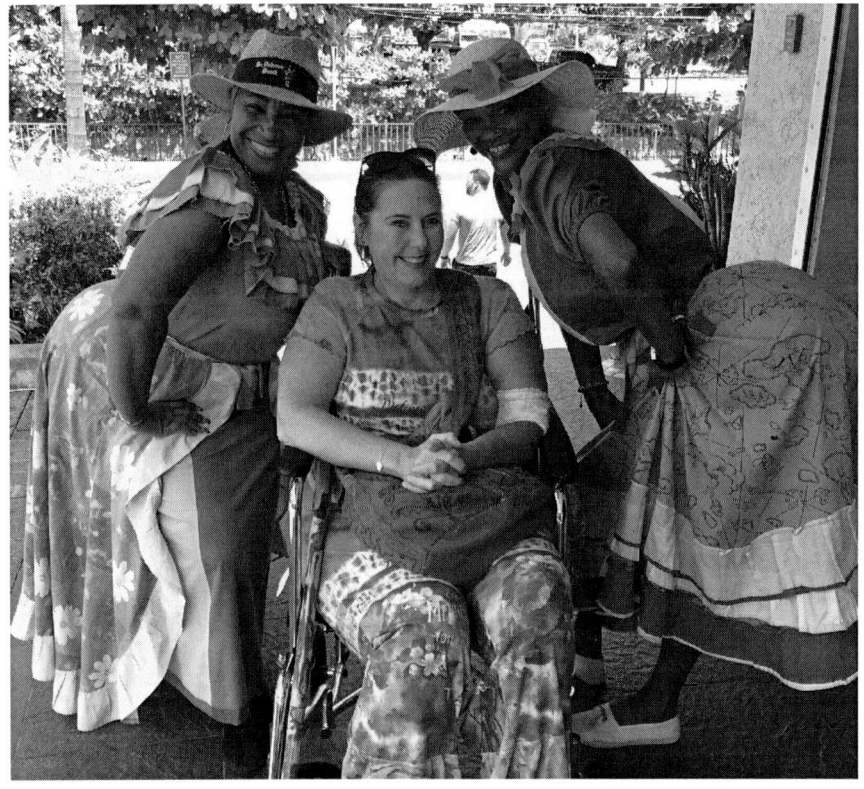

Jamaica 2015

During the month of April in 2015, I decided to break free and go on a fourteen-day cruise to the Caribbean and Panama. My friend Stacy accompanied me and we were able to explore Guatemala, Nicaragua, Costa Rica, Columbia,

Honduras, Panama, Key West, Mexico, and the Bahamas. I have to admit, much of this trip has been forgotten because of my poor cognition and memory loss. I could ask Stacy what we did and where we went, but that is not the focus of this book. My message to my readers is to understand how debilitating Lyme life is for everyone involved.

St. Croix 2015

The things that I do remember were the incredible food, entertainment, and cultural experiences I had enjoyed, all the while stuck in a transport wheelchair. We stayed in a very nice room in the concierge section of the Regatta Cruise Ship from the Oceana Cruises Line, a very foodie ship. We attended trivia contests, lectures, movies, and musical events onboard the ship. I remember traveling, but not much of what we did onshore.

Medical Team on Panama Cruise 2015

The only things I do remember crystal clear was my PICC line flush maintenance and dressing changes on the ship. I have no idea why these memories remain intact, but they do. I had to take it very easy on the ship, especially with my poor stamina, poor balance, increased fatigue, and pain. Stacy was a gem carting my ass around and tending to my needs. She is as independent as I am so she was not upset when I could not participate in all the ship activities; she just did her own thing. Since I could not stand and walk on the ship, I was very creative with my personal hygiene. I would work out twice a week in the gym and have my hair washed in the salon. Because my sensitivity to touch was mounting, I bowed out of any massages.

At that time on the ship, I enjoyed being away from home and not infusing antibiotics. I remained on all of my oral medications and tinctures, but I knew that once I got home, I had to resume my infusions. This was always in the back of my mind. Hopefully, I will be able to return again. We became friends with Captain Hanson from Norway and enjoyed listening to his stories. We were easily recognized because of my wheelchair. I had brain fog, so once a person told me their name, it would go in one ear and out the other. So I would smile and pretend I knew who the hell I was speaking with and acknowledge everything they said.

French Chef on Panama Cruise 2015

Working out on Panama Cruise 2015

Chapter Ten
Office Consultation Lyme Disease Follow Up

Yesterday, I had my first Zithromax infusion in two weeks. Bridget came and changed my dressing and then I started the IV antibiotic drip into my heart. The all-too-familiar nausea and dizziness reemerged. Then I slept for three hours—it was only eleven o'clock in the morning. Thank goodness I was still in my pajamas.

Today, I traveled to Albany. It was a very tough appointment. We discussed my cruise and all the challenges and limitations that arose. It was very depressing. Then we got to the meat of the matter—more absolutely crazy debilitating symptoms—some old, some brand spanking new. The list included fatigue, daily migraines, left ankle pain, entire back pain, and the top clincher—loss of hearing! I knew my hearing was getting bad, but I thought it was due to all the rock concerts I went to when I was younger. However, much to my surprise, it was due to Lyme. I saw people talking and at times could not hear them. Other times I could not comprehend what they were saying. Jen told me that I was displaying expressive word aphasia, meaning I could not say what I was thinking and this also displayed by stuttering. I had never stuttered in my life and now I was full-fledged stutterer! It was very embarrassing and annoying. When we went through the Lyme symptom assessment questions, the results all suggested that I did better on the IV antibiotics than off them. So I began again with my tri-weekly infusions.

Jen suggested that I contact a colleague and practitioner of hers, Art Smuckler, who was a pedorthist. Art made orthotics for people who had problems walking and was very well known in the Albany area so I agreed to see him. I was still seeing my podiatrist, but nothing was helping my ambulation. The benefit of seeking the help of the pedorthist is that their main focus is fitting, adapting, modifying, and fabricating footwear to structurally promote healthier gait. I hoped that Art would help me walk better or at least walk.

My new diagnoses were: muscular skeletal pain, pain in joint unspecified, and headaches. An EKG was also administered and a thyroid lab test was ordered. I decided I wanted to try to get disability insurance and needed copies of all medical testing and notes to present to the government. I never knew it was going to get this bad. I could not work, live, or just plain exist without help. My Blue Cross Blue Shield insurance covered nothing except for medication and nursing care after I had reached a hefty deductible.

To make a long story short, I made an appointment with Social Security for an appointment to discuss disability benefits. Mary Kay accompanied me to the Federal Building in Syracuse and was able to maneuver me in my transport wheelchair through the metal detector and up to the top floor. I thought I had this disability thing in the bag! Along with my notes from Dr. Stram, I was also able to gather all notes from Dr. Cornish, plus my completed Social Security questionnaire. We waited two hours for my appointment that lasted fifteen minutes, and I was denied! I was too sick and tired to be angry and it was time to find an attorney.

Chapter Eleven
Year of the PICC

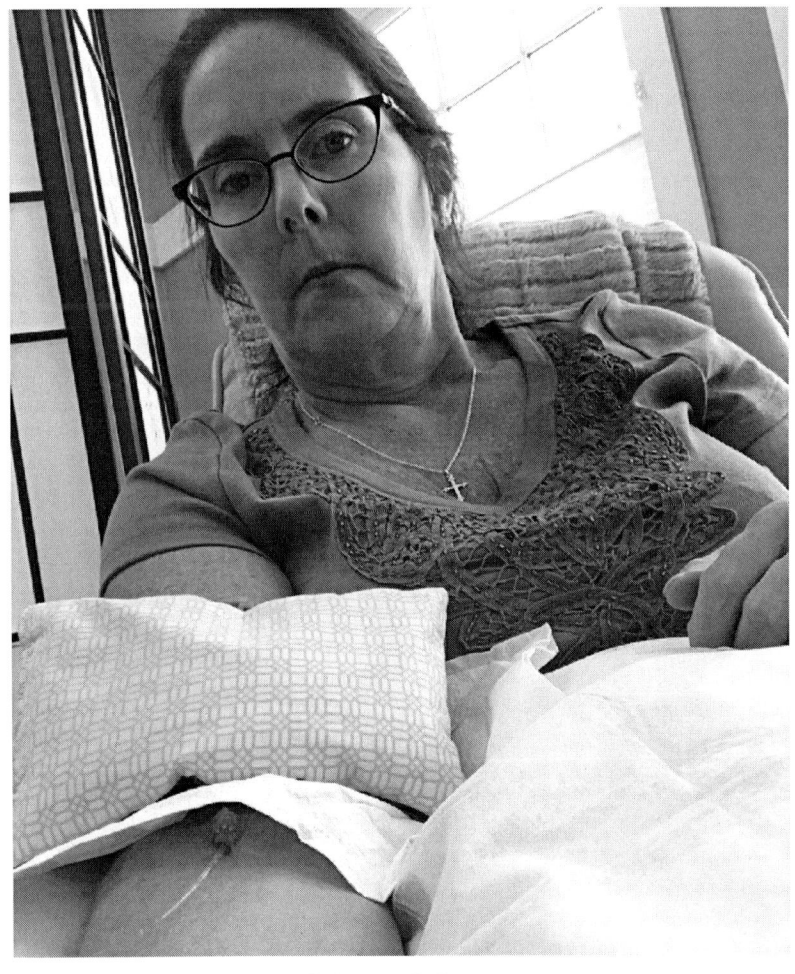

Receiving Infusions

This year, I had five comprehensive appointments at The Stram Center in May, June, September, November, and December. It was full of a lot of ups and downs managing the ongoing changes with medications, diet and nutrition sensitivity issues, severe herxing, and a constant need for outside help to manage my life at home. Ever since I was young, I have been a very independent person and adapting to the need to ask for help was completely foreign to me. Thus, asking for help was like pulling teeth. I soon realized that I had to let go of my pride and accept help.

It was quite a turn of events. I was able to get all IV therapies such as: Myers Cocktail, NAC, and straight Glutathione all through my PICC line. This made life so much easier and accessible for nurses and me. No more IV pokes and missed veins! Since Dr. Stram had built a new facility right down the road from his post-stamp-sized office that had a huge infusion room with ten infusion chairs, life was good. The nurses even had an office for themselves.

Fatigue was the worst that it had been in years and mainly due to the toxins in my system as a result of all antibiotics being ingested and infused. Every visit to The Stram Center required a driver, so I would beg and plead with my friends and family to drive me and luckily, someone would always come through for me. This is why I would ask for as many IV therapies that would help with detoxifying my liver. These therapies are not for the faint of heart. Infusing with antibiotics made me ill and the removal of the toxins made me even sicker. However, this was the course of treatment I asked for and at this stage of the game, it was the best protocol for Lyme treatment at the time.

My main concerns this year were a combination of the past three years, amplified by ten thousand. Poor proprioception, neuropathy, and chronic pain were at the top of the list. I went to the gym and walked the track with my walker, went to acupuncture, ate a clean diet, took my medications, got sufficient sleep, went to a pedorthist, and wear custom made orthotics, but I still couldn't feel my feet and legs or walk. My digestion was off the charts—a complete mess. I ate gluten free, sugar free, and dairy free, but still experienced diarrhea, constipation, sluggish stools, little to no appetite, weight gain and loss, and horrific gastric pain. My rage and anger was constant, along with having to live through the holiday season without a scowl on my face. My brain fog, word aphasia, getting lost driving, and experiencing daily confusion with everything and everyone was the icing on the cake.

I made it through every infusion, every fit of rage, and every muscle spasm like a champ. This damn disease would not get the best of me and I will make it through every treatment, every setback, and everything that causes me inconceivable pain and emotional upset. My hair was falling out and my hairdresser's choice of colorants was causing my scalp to burn and flake off. I looked like hell, but I was a fighter, rearing on the inside like a Leo. I will make it through this hell.

The following are my diagnosis for this year:

- Unspecified arthropathy unspecified site
- Migraine unspecified not intractable
- Myalgia, and myositis unspecified
- Sciatica
- Joint pain unspecified
- Unspecified Malaise/fatigue

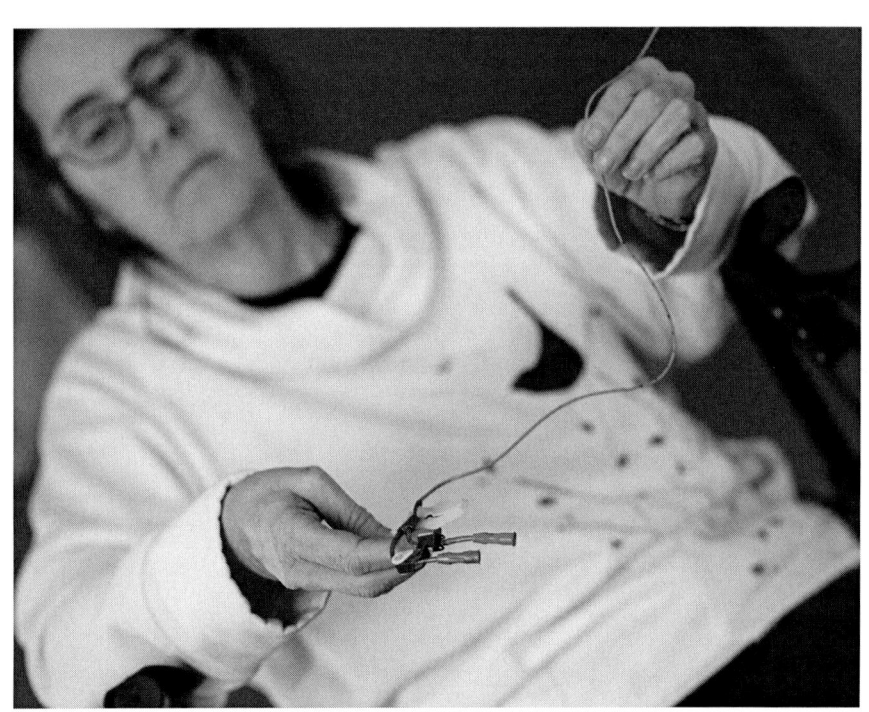

PICC Line

Chapter Twelve
Take a Deep Breath and Hold it!

> "The time has come," the Walrus said,
> "To talk of many things:
> Of shoes—and ships—and sealing-wax—
> Of cabbages—and kings—
> And why the sea is boiling hot—
> And whether pigs have wings."

Lewis Carroll writes this in his work, *The Walrus and the Carpenter*. I couldn't tell you why this phrase popped into my noodle at this stage of the game, but it did. Maybe I was feeling that this life was like living in a game set, like Lewis Carroll described where I ate this and drank that while feeling tall or small and always fearing that the dreaded red queen would chop off my head. Yes, this is how I thought about life and still do. Life is a whirlwind of emotions, thoughts, fears, resentments—you name it—and for me, always out of my control. Regaining what I had lost was and is always in the front of my mind. It is always depressing to think about what I had become: a recluse, an invalid, an angry soul.

This year, 2016, brought a little freedom back to my life. After a year and two weeks of being tethered to an IV pole, having a tube connected directly to my heart, I was going to be set free. The main thing that came to mind was that I could take a shower without wrapping up the PICC in the tight plastic sleeve with the fear of it getting wet. Yes, freedom! All I had to do was take a deep breath and hold it! I was ready, willing, and able to get it out. We discussed the removal at length with the doctor after I stopped the IV antibiotics, in case I needed to go back on them. A problem arose when antibiotics were discontinued. My IV management company protocol for PICC line maintenance did not include pushing daily Heparin in my line, only saline solution. In order to keep a clean line since saline alone does not prevent clots from forming, Heparin was used to prevent clots. This was immediately brought to Dr. Stram's attention so he shared his concern with the maintenance company and Heparin was added. I was relieved with this outcome.

On January 14, 2016, I was headed to Delmar for my comprehensive appointment and IV NAC infusion via my PICC line. Luckily, a new Lyme friend, Steve, drove me and attended my appointment to see if he would like to receive Lyme treatment from The Stram Center. Since I have been going to The Stram Center, I have referred many people manifested with Lyme symptoms to explore the possibility of them having Lyme. Steve and I ate lunch at Peaches Café in Albany and traveled on to Delmar. My appointment went the same as before, discussing symptoms, accomplishments, and fallbacks. It was the same old stuff discussed. Now it was onto the NAC infusion.

When I was seeing Dr. Cornish between 2012-2014, I received NAC infusions that helped increase my Glutathione levels and liver detoxing. I was ready to work on that issue again. I really loved going to The Stram Center because when I came up with ideas for my treatment, they listened to me and actually implemented them. After four years of Lyme treatment and intense research, I had very well thought out ideas for a creative protocol. So here we are again, NAC—the amino acid that helps the gut and immune system! After my appointment, I headed for the infusion room to receive my dose. I climbed up the stairs and found my coveted chair and had my vitals taken. After Bridget completed the vitals, she asked me if I was ready to have my PICC removed. I could not believe my ears! I had no idea that today was the day for me to be free! She went over the removal instructions: take a very deep breath and hold it for twenty seconds. She explained that this would aid in an easier removal due to no movement in my chest. I agreed.

Tears started to flow and I became overwhelmingly emotional. I do not know why this occurred; maybe it had been a part of my identity for such a long time. Things were changing again for me. Before it was removed, Bridget administered the NAC, and as usual, it caused a large amount of herxing. So I had my last infusion while thinking about the removal. Bridget unhooked the long IV tube to my PICC and prepped for the removal dressed in sterile paper outfit, plastic full-faced mask, and gloves. I practiced holding my breath and stayed still. Bridget removed the dressing and asked me to hold my breath again. One, two, three, and then a very long, 43 cm to be exact, purple, plastic tube emerged from my arm. It was amazing to see this tube that carried medicine into my body that had saved my life; it was placed in a plastic bag and I brought it home—it was my badge of courage. We traveled home and upon arrival I took the longest shower that I had taken in a year! Today was a very good day.

Chapter Thirteen
What Was I Really Doing?

Over the next year, I went to The Stram six times to receive NAC, Glutathione and Meyers Cocktail therapies. The appointment dates for comprehensive exams and infusions included: March 4, April 14, April 29, May 13, June 24, August 4, and October 10. As the year played out, I would receive an exam and NAC infusion. The next visit, I would just receive an infusion and then alternate. My oral medications and natural supplements remained the same and I was still suffering from: fatigue, malaise, migraine, tachycardia, neuropathy, and pain. Another thing that remained the same was my consistent diagnosis of Lyme disease.

During this intensive infusion protocol, I knew that I was improving, especially my immune system and gut. However, many symptoms remained the same. What would it take for me to feel my feet again, walk on my own, or even ski? I had no idea when any of this would occur or it was even possible to think that I would become whole again. Since in treatment, I had traveled to Bali, Mexico, and even Canyon Ranch in Arizona for healing. I searched everywhere I could to heal, from mental health practitioners to psychic mediums to traditional healers. This journey, both physically and mentally, was getting pretty old.

In October, a few things changed. I stopped the infusions and all medications and I shared this with Jen and Dr. Stram. It is important to note that they didn't give up on me. They knew I needed a break so I did not see them again until January, 2017. I also needed a holiday break too—no medications or restrictions over the holidays resulted in many emotional and physical problems so when January came, it was time for my next appointment in Delmar and I hoped to receive some relief.

• • •

The following is an excerpt from my Lyme diary:

Questionnaire Interview
Are you globally feeling better, worse or the same?
This past few months have been full of ups and downs. During December I was severely depressed so much that my therapist was very concerned about my well-being. In January, things turned around and I have been feeling better. The dysthymia turned into malaise and it's much easier to live my life. Emotionally, I'm a little better. Physically, about the same except for less pain.
What are the most prominent symptoms currently?
Neuropathy, poor proprioception, right leg and hip pain, migraines, severe foot pain in the morning, fatigue, depression.
What symptoms have you noticed changed for better or worse?
Better: Mood, dysthymia, Worse: sleep vagal nerve? Every night.
Nothing was really working so I decided to start a new herbal protocol created by Dr. Lee Cowden who utilized NeutraMedix herbal supplements to treat Lyme disease. It consisted of around twenty-four different tinctures and two capsules. The combination of herbals changed every thirteen days and lasted nine months. It was a very tedious journey. Every three hours, I would put drops of herbs into a glass of filtered water every day. I would plan my day for the proper timing for my supplement intake. It was a lot like having a PICC. Just to let you know, herbal antimicrobials are much more intense than pharmaceutical antibiotics. This protocol would attack the bacteria for the front door, back door, and side door. They would alter their appearance so that the bacteria could not identify them and treat more than one co-infection at once. It was intense, affordable, and helped me restart my healing process. The medicinal marijuana was still working and helped keep the chronic pain at bay.

The following was from next April:

- Are you globally feeling better, worse or the same?
- Since January, I have been on the new Cowden protocol and have been doing very well.
- What are most prominent symptoms currently?
- Neuropathy, poor proprioception, fatigue after herx.
- What symptoms have noticed change for better or worse?
- Mood, sleep, appetite, stamina, and rage better. Anxiety has increased, memory still poor, isolation causing problems, and family and friend issues because no one believes me.

I had one more phone appointment with Jen in the spring and discussed my progress. She wanted to see me in six months and to call if I needed anything. I agreed. This time around I was a slave to Dr. Cowden.

the Cowden Protocol

John of God

Chapter Fourteen
John of God

You know how things can turn full circle? Well, an emerging memory changed my life. In 2008, I was watching an episode of *Oprah* when she was interviewing a man named João Teixeira de Faria from Abadiânia, Brazil. For us in the United States, he is better known as John of God. From the age of six, John has been healing individuals and curing many illnesses. He is a devout Christian and Catholic who allows God to work through him. He also works with metaphysical beings called the Entities of light who are also referred to as ascended masters. Many of the Entities that manifest through John are saints and holy beings. John's patron saint of his *casa* is St. Ignatius of Loyola. When I was in California at Nine Gates Mystery School, John of God was a hot topic and I knew he traveled to other countries including the United States. I was very intrigued so I ordered a book by his translator, Heather Cummings, to check him out.

    John suffered many years of prosecution and even experienced incardination for his healing practices, but continued to do God's work and provide help to everyone who needed healing. As the years went on, he was healing people everywhere he traveled. He eventually became well known and people traveled from all over the world to meet him and experience healing. Since John only spoke Portuguese, he needed translators to help him with the numerous guests who traveled to his *casa*. Heather Cummings is one of the translators who travels to the states with him, since she owns a place of her own near John's home. Some of my friends stayed with Heather while getting healing from John while in Brazil. I decided I needed to visit John of God on his next visit to the states.

In October of 2016 and 2017, I was able to attend three-day events at the Omega Institute in Rhinebeck, New York for the John of God healing experience. There were many rules and protocols that had to be followed and I was prepared to do what I needed to heal. I was ready once more. We had to dress in white, refrain from all electronics, and eat simply. The white clothing was said to allow the Entities of light to view auras, the body's energy field, and help form a diagnosis for healing. Steering clear from electronics will allow the Entities' healing frequencies to create harmony in the body and promote the healing process. Since we would be doing a lot of physical and emotional cleansing and detoxifying, a clean diet was a must.

My friend Natalie accompanied me to my first visit to see John of God and receive healing. We shared a motel room in Rhinebeck that was only fifteen minutes from the Omega Institute and very easy to find. We arrived the night before the event to make sure we were on time for the first meeting. I had made plans to meet Gregg Kirk, the president of a Lyme disease group, called "Ticked Off Foundation", the first day. Gregg works with many Lyme patients and brings groups to Brazil, while providing counseling and treating them holistically with reiki, tinctures, and energy work. When Natalie and I arrived at Omega at 7:30 in the morning, we were hustled through the lobby area and picked up our paper tricolored bracelets depicting the three days we were attending. After that, we were able to hop onto a golf cart that transported handicapped visitors to the event tent. I saw three small tents and a huge tent amidst a sea of white-clothed people. The first tent was an infirmary space, the second and third housed an information table and John of God holy water. The largest tent was large enough to hold over four thousand people and the first day was at maximum capacity!

I was very thirsty so I bought a bottle of holy water and an Omega bag and we quickly got to our seats inside the large tent in the handicapped section. Before we saw John of God, Heather arrived at the front of the tent, picked up a microphone, and spoke to the crowd about John of God and his many accomplishments along with directions for our healings, called Interventions. In Brazil, the healings are called surgeries and in the states they are called Interventions. So the first thing we did was be presented in front of John and allow the Entities to see our issues that needed adjustment. This was done in a separate building. Everything ran like clockwork and was extremely fluid in motion. The next step was to receive the Intervention so we returned to the same building and sat with our eyes closed and our hands on our hearts. The group remained silent, listening attentively to the *casa* sisters giving us instructions. We then heard and felt Entities; John entered the building, breathing heavily and shuffling his feet. I desperately wanted to peek, but I did not. There was a deep vibration in my body starting from my root chakra or my tailbone heading all the way up to crown chakra, or the top of my head. Having Lyme, I experienced tremors for years and this was a different vibration. It was kind of like things inside of me were opening up and expanding. I felt lighter and calmer. This lasted for about fifteen minutes and we were escorted out and led to another tent where we received more information and about what to do next. We were instructed to go back to our hotel and sleep as long as we could without speaking or using the phone, computer, or television. I missed Gregg the first day, but knew that I would see him tomorrow. We were told to arrive at 2:30 P.M. the next day because we would need sleep and sleep we did! Natalie and I slept for thirteen hours straight! We were not hungry or thirsty.

The next day, we met Gregg and a few of his friends receiving Interventions to help with Lyme disease issues. We all headed into the large tent and went into the Intervention building. I experienced the same things at this Intervention and returned back to the hotel to sleep. The next day, we returned at 1:30 P.M. and prepared for our final Intervention. Before entering the large tent, I ordered three cases of John of God holy water to take home. Something incredible happened during this Intervention. While I was seated in my chair with my eyes closed and hands on my heart, I asked the Entities to see what I was supposed to see, hear what I was supposed to hear, and feel what I was supposed to feel. At that moment, I felt a large pop in my right ear and a warming sensation.

When we departed from the Intervention, I was a little dizzy and found a bench to sit on outside of the building. Gregg, his friends, Natalie, and I chatted about our experience. I was having a difficulty with a few things and motioned to Natalie to come over to me so I could ask a question. I told her that I could not remember her speaking so much. I then realized that I could hear everything everyone was saying without straining to listen. I got my hearing back that I lost due to Lyme! I had a miracle! I was believer.

In seven days, I was instructed to prepare for stitch removal from the Entities as a result of the spiritual Interventions. This process happened between 1 A.M. and 5 A.M. in the morning. I was instructed to dress in white and have a glass of holy water next to my bed to be drunk in the morning upon waking up. Stitch removal occurred after each Intervention and sometimes I awakened when the stitches were removed and witnessed the Entities at work. It was not scary at all; it was God at work through John. I saw a miracle being preforming on me in front of my very eyes!

The following year, I returned to the Omega Institute and attended John's event. The first day, thirty-seven hundred people were there. Wow! I have never seen anything like this in my life—another sea of white! The Entities only offered two Interventions this time due to the crowd's high vibrations. The first day, I received an Intervention and I returned back to the hotel in Hyde Park and had a very difficult time sleeping. The second day, I met up with Gregg and his friend Justin and prepared for our blessing from John of God.

Something strange and different happened this day. When we were settled for the blessing in the Interventions building, we had our eyes closed, hands on our hearts and we witnessed a miracle. I heard two loud bangs and a message in Portuguese translated by Heather, "Open your eyes, John of God wants you to open your eyes and look." I saw a man who used crutches to walk walking without them. When John walked by me he gave me a stern look and went on his way. John of God took the man around the Intervention building to the outside tent for everyone to witness the miracle. I was sobbing and overwhelmed by what I had just witnessed.

The next day, I experienced something even more incredible. Upon arriving at the Omega at 7:30 in the morning, I was a little jittery. I arrived early at the large tent and worked on balancing my chakras. Deep in thought, I did not even see Gregg arrive and sit next to me while I was preparing for my Intervention. I was able to get halfway to the crown chakra before heading into the Intervention building. Gregg and I were not seated together which I found rather odd, but I sat where I was instructed to sit. I remained with my walker near a table and not in the main group of folding chairs. When I was settled,

I continued with my chakra balancing and managed to get to the crown. I then became angry and something took over; I demanded the Entities to fix me, make me whole—let me walk! Then, I asked for forgiveness and abandoned my petty pride. All of a sudden, I started growling, hissing, and spitting. A *casa* sister and brother came over to help with the negative entity removal as I growled and fought with them. After two minutes or so, I stopped that behavior and was calm until the shaking started. At first, it was my hands and then it went systemic. I had a full-blown seizure! After the seizure, I was whisked off to an infirmary where ten mediums kept silent space. I was lifted from my walker to a cot and had my shoes taken off before I lay down. I rested for forty-five minutes before I left for the hotel. When I was driving, I called Gregg to see how he was doing. He said that he was already in bed and thought he heard me growling during the Intervention. I told him that I also had a seizure. He said that I was hyperventilating in the large tent while I was preparing for the Intervention. He then congratulated me for my healing. I slept very well that night and returned home the following day.

Chapter Fifteen
Follow Up Office Consultation Lyme Disease

In 2017, I decided to leave my new primary physician in Syracuse because of his disillusion that I was still not sick with Lyme disease and that I just complained a lot. It was the same old story and just a different day. So I made a decision to ask Jen and Dr. Stram to become my primary physician and nurse and they agreed. I knew that they were planning to build an office in Syracuse and I could be transferred to them when it came to fruition. This appointment was a little intense because I had to receive a physical, go over six months' worth of symptoms, and review my extensive lab results from my twelve-vial blood draw two weeks prior. This time, I also received a Myers Cocktail and Glutathione push after my appointment.

The notes from my journal were as follows:
May - October 2017

- Are you globally feeling better, worse or the same?
  Over the past six months, I have been improving in a few areas—cognition, memory, rage (at times), sleep, digestion, energy (at times). The areas that are staying the same are lack of mobility, pain (better with the medicinal marijuana), internal fill body spasms at night, increased isolation.

- What are most prominent symptoms currently?
  Neuropathy, poor proprioception, right leg and hip pain, mi-

graines, fatigue, depression, internal muscle spasms at night, hand and jaw tremors, teeth grinding at night, brain fog, teary-eyed many times for no reason, small scabs on my back and chest.

- What symptoms have noticed changed for better or worse? Better: hip/foot pain, digestion, Worse: no appetite, at times horrible aphasia that causes escalating rage.

- Are you having any gastrointestinal pain or discomfort? None—I try to have a clean diet.

- Are you experiencing any issues with yeast? No.

- Notes:
  I finally bought a customized wheelchair—it makes it a little easier to get around at the mall and at the fair. I have been on the Cowden protocol over the past nine months and during certain protocols, herxing was severe—migraines, fatigue, increased pain, sleep issues, urination issues brain fog.

I was going to PT twice a week now it's once a week for insurance reasons; I decreased workout to three times a week instead of four and have a massage once a week. Art, my pedorthist, is still helping with my orthotics and encouraged me to start writing a book about my journey.

Poor proprioception and neuropathy are my main issues that I struggle with. People say how they understand my issues, but if you don't have what I have, you don't. I am learning so much about myself as I write my book and can't believe how far I have come, yet I have a long way to go.

We discussed the intense herxes that I was experiencing at night with the internal tremors, increased leg pain, and muscle spasms that were all caused by the co-infection, Bartonella. I was finally ready to get back to work and start aggressively treating my illness again. Since I had not visited The Stram

Center in the past six months, I was able to save up for a few consecutive visits. Jen and I discussed my experience utilizing the Cowden Protocol that did fairly well, but needed more help with my symptoms. Jen suggested that I use a natural herbal tincture protocol to address my specific Bartonella symptoms and I agreed whole-heartedly. It consisted of an antimicrobial and detoxification supplement. We reviewed my extensive lab work and saw that I still had issues with my Thyroid Gland, low vitamin D3, and a new positive for Epstein Barr, but still negative across the board for Lyme disease and all of its co-infections. So we had a lot to address and I was ready again to get my life back. My diagnoses were pretty interesting this time around: Lyme disease, malaise and fatigue, essential l and other forms of tremors, spasms of muscles, myalgia, and myositis. In other words, it means Lyme, fatigue, spasms, pain, pain, and more pain. Even though I had a clinical presentation of Lyme disease, the lab results from the testing sources in United States did not detect the Lyme bacteria, Borrelia Burgdorferi.

My Myers Cocktail took two hours to infuse because of my hypersensitivity of the herxes from the intense detoxification and the Glutathione push. When I left The Stram Center, I was a little groggy from the infusion so I sat in my car for about an hour to prepare for my drive home. I had done this on many occasions so it was old hat to me. When I got home, I slept for twelve hours straight. The long day and herbal medications took a toll on me. The next morning, I woke up well rested and prepared myself for new tinctures and medication schedule. I put aside all my leftover Cowden tinctures and stored them for my friend, Cindy, who was already using the protocol and replaced them with the new tinctures. I was all set and ready to go!

The next day, I prepared my tincture decoction, starting with a drop each of the antimicrobial and detoxification tinctures added to a small glass of John of God water. These herbs were bitter, but knew I would get accustomed to the taste. The first night after I started the new protocol, I actually slept through the night without a spasm of any kind. Each day, I added a drop of each to my protocol until I reached thirty drops. As the days went on, I felt how the herbs that I took twice a day were affecting me. My fatigue increased along with my hip pain, insomnia, and loss of appetite. Each day was worse than the previous day. It was Thanksgiving weekend and I knew that I had to wait to contact Dr. Stram about how he wanted me to handle my symptoms this time around. He would probably want to start Burbur and Pinella Brain Cleanse again, along with parsley or possibly increase my probiotics, but you never know, he may have something else up his sleeve to help me.

The fatigue was getting worse and when I left the house I had to use my wheelchair. Even in my chair, my energy faded rather quickly. It was rather disappointing, but I was familiar with course of different treatment modalities and just went along with the flow; I had no other choice.

Chapter Sixteen
"A Separate Reality"

My life today is a different reality. I look at the person who I was, who I am today, and who I will be in the future. When doing this, I question how I see myself and explore how others see me. In one word, it is a conundrum. When I think about my identity, I am at a loss for words. Before Lyme, I was happily married and was a successful artist and therapist. I went out with friends, attended local music events, skied, ran, and traveled throughout the world. Things are so different now and I struggle to find myself and who I will become.

One thing I know is that I did not like who I had become. I see myself as a victim who struggles daily with chronic pain and fights with the construct of being handicapped for life. Was I a drug addict or just plain lazy or even going crazy? I have no idea. Some of the words that describe me today are potter, daughter, sister, aunt, nerd, author, artist, or seer. These are the ones that first come to mind and there are more. Who am I really?

Carlos Castinada, a California reporter who interviewed the Mexican shaman, Don Juan, wrote about all of his experiences he had with him. During their conversations, they spoke a lot about identity, self-worth, and finding themselves. He wrote a book called *A Separate Reality* that delves into different facets of how we see and perceive the world around us. I am a lot like Carlos when he was trying to find his reality and not his perceived reality. What is real and what is imagined? Would I always be sick and in pain? Would I ever walk again on my own? Would I ever allow love into my life again? Would I ever truly love myself again? Would I ever accept myself as a whole person? I cannot tell you; I have no idea and really do not care.

The flip side of all this confusion is how other people see me. The non-Lyme physicians think I'm crazy and a complainer. Most of my friends have dropped off the face of the earth and are no longer in my life. Some family and friends who did stick around are confused about what I am doing and/or experiencing. Neighbors think that I am a recluse and call me a unicorn because they don't think I'm real. However, the most important thing I notice is when onlookers view me, they see a healthy-looking woman who looks and sometimes acts healthy, but has problems walking, speaking, hearing, and becomes overwhelmed easily.

So what is MY reality? I hope to see myself as a strong person. Many of my friends and acquaintances see me as a Lyme warrior and someone who can take on the world. To tell you the truth, I do feel strong some days, but those days are far and few between. Most days are bleak and miserable, but a few aren't that bad. It is all about adaptability and how I can creatively change the way I view and live in my present reality. I hope to find a healthy balance of accepting my limitations and rejoice in my small accomplishments. Allowing God into my daily life has slowly helped me accept a few things in my life, although I still get angry at Him and confused as to why He wants me to be sick and in pain. I truly know that I was not picked out to be chronically ill; it was just the luck of the draw. The following is one of my favorite lyrics Neil Young's song "Old Man":

> "Don't let it bring you down
> It's only castles burning
> Find someone who's turning
> And you will come around"

I recently was reading a book of psalms and prayers and came across the Prayer of St. Francis. Extremely moved, I read it over and over again, embracing each word as a symbol of my journey—not just my Lyme journey, but rather, my life journey. Maybe this is what I need to focus on now. It is similar to what Neil Young is speaking about in his song, "Old Man." To me, it is all about a change in attitude and focus.

"The Prayer of St. Francis"

Make me a channel of your peace.
Where there is hatred, let me bring your love.
Where there is injury, your pardon, Lord,
And where there's doubt, true faith in you.

Make me a channel of your peace.
Where there's despair in life, let me bring hope.
Where there is darkness only light,
And where there's sadness ever joy.

Oh Master, grant that I may never seek
So much to be consoled as to console.
To be understood as to understand,
To be loved as to love with all my soul.

Make me a channel of your peace.
It is in pardoning that we are pardoned;
In giving of ourselves that we receive,
And in dying that we're born to eternal life.

I have lived in the dark for such a long time, not knowing the root cause of many of my problems, and obstacles that have caused me so much pain and discomfort have slowly dissipated. I am able to forge ahead and share what I have learned with anyone struggling as I have struggled. I hope to see the world with clearer, happier, and accepting eyes. My personal goals still include becoming healthier physically, emotionally, and spiritually.

ILADS and Lyme Conference

Dr. Daniel Cameron, ILADS conference 2016

Dr. Heidi Puk, ILADS conference 2016

Dennis Schoen, founder of Research Nutritionals, ILADS Conference 2013

NYS Fair Lyme booth with Eva Haughie 2013

Chittenango Lyme Protest 2014

NYS Fair

NYS Fair

Bali

Receiving Baptism, 2011

Bali sister, Kim, 2012

My friend Made at the Water Temple, 2012

Made, Hindu Priest and Gay with Ceremonial Temple Gift, 2012

Mother Temple with Priest, 2011

Elephant Sactuary. 2012

My Family Throughout the Years

Mark and Pat Conan, Mom and Dad

Dancing with Tim, brother 1994

Margaret, niece, age one

Christmas with Tim and Margaret

Mark, Brother

Patsy, sister, Mack, nephew in Chicago

Margot Jacoby, Cousin

Medical and Holistic Practices and Practitioners

Arthur Smuckler, Pedorthist

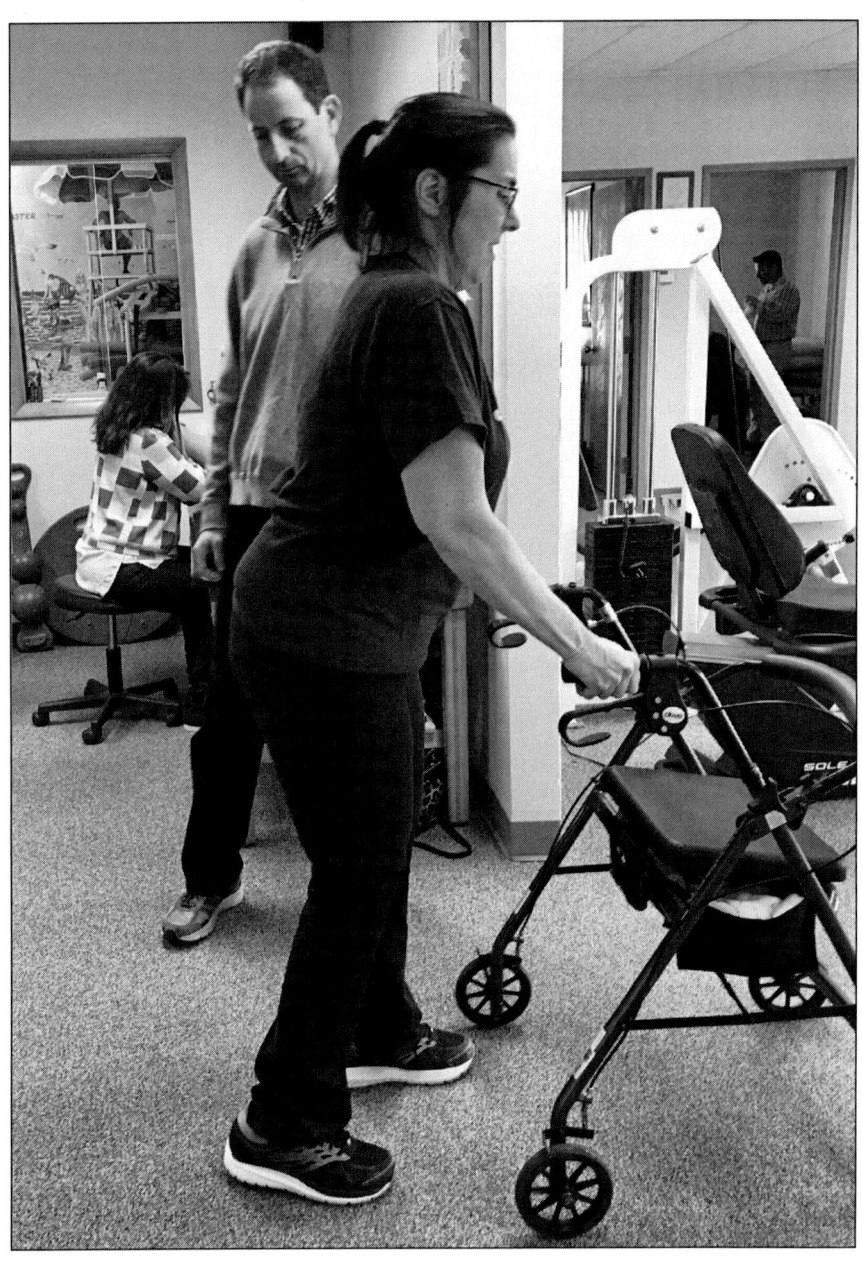

Physical Therapy with Martin Canavan PT

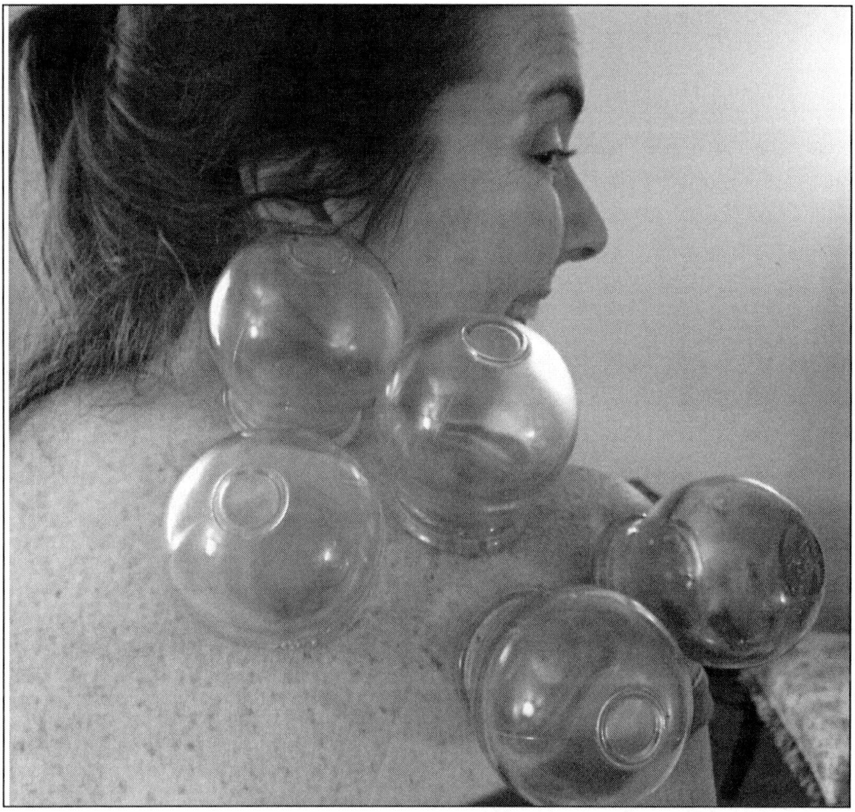

Chinese Cupping

Deborah Jones, Nine Gate Mystery School

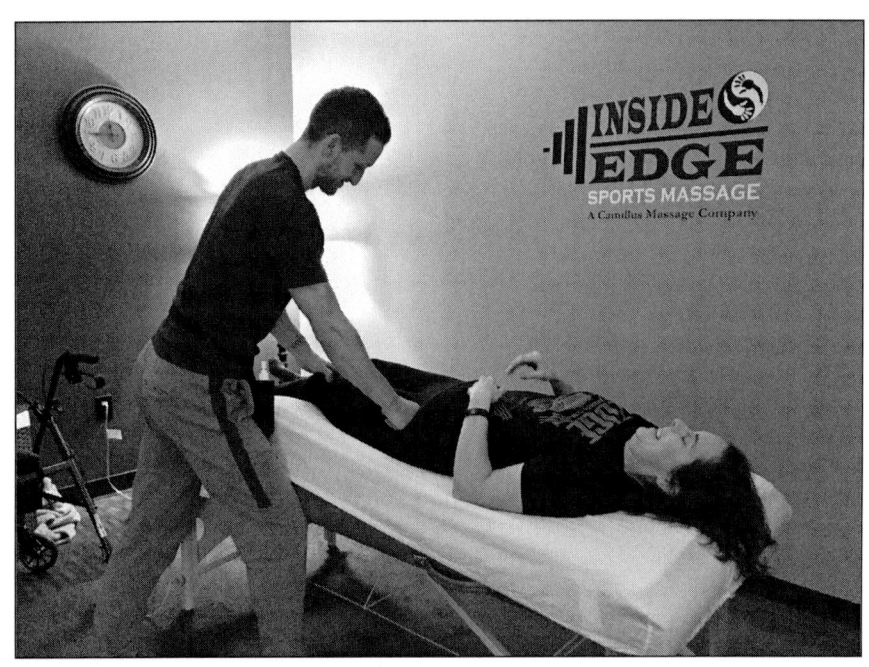

Massage Therapy with Kyle Carleo

Megan Wagner, Kabala Teacher

Mark Saito, Kahuna

Working Out at Edge Gym

Angry Day

Gym Tribe

Pushing the Sled

Walk training with my trainer Pete Haley

Kyle Carleo, MT and Pete Haley at Edge Gym

Vacations

The Coonans in Tipperary, Ireland 1995

Stonehenge 1995

Cliffs of Moher, Ireland 1995

Vermont 1998

Lenny and Ginny Obergfell in Cancun, Mexico 2009

Miami Zoo 2014

Alaska 2015

Von Trapp Brewery, Vermont 2016

Resources

Physicians/Practitioners/Nursing
    Dr. EboniCornish: (703) 709-1119
    Dr. Daniel Cameron: (914) 666-4665
    Coram Healthcare – (315) 425-8028 Infusion Specialists
    Karen Dellas, LAC (315) 439-2194 Licensed Acupuncturist
    Mark Fohs LMHC (315) 422-2134 Licensed Mental Health Therapist
    Medical Registry (315) 468-3239 Nursing Registry
    Arthur Smuckler PED (518) 869-0021Pedorthist
    Jennifer Goldstock NP 518-218-4455

Organizations
    Alabama Lyme Disease Association: (334) 625-1023
    American Lyme Disease Foundation: www.aldf.com
    Arizona Lyme Disease Association: www.azlyme.org/
    Bay Area Lyme Foundation: https://www.bayarealyme.org
    CNLADS - Canadian National Lyme and Associated Diseases Society www.facebook.com/JJShakti/
    Canadian Lyme Disease Foundation: +1 250-768-0978
    CNY Lyme Suppport – Facebook
    Empire State Lyme Disease Association: www.empirestatelymediseaseas-sociation.org
    Empire State Lyme Disease Organization of Onondaga County (315) 254-1548 Facebook
    Florida Lyme Disease Association: www.flda.org

Hudson Valley Healing Arts Center: Horowitz Richard MD: (845) 229-8977

Global Lyme Alliance: www.globallymealliance.org

ILADS: www.ilads.org

Kentucky Lyme Disease Association Lyme support group Louisville, KY www.kentuckylymedisease.org/

Lyme Association of Greater KC: (913) 438-5963

Lyme Disease Association: www.lymediseaseassociation.org

Lyme Disease Association of Australia: www.lymedisease.org.au

Lyme Disease Association of Southeastern Pennsylvania: www.lymepa.org

Lyme Disease Network: www.lymenet.org

Lyme Disease Organization: www.lymedisease.org

LymeLight Foundation: www.lymelightfoundation.org

Lyme Disease Treatment Grants

Lyme Ontario: lymeontario.com

Lyme Warriors: lymewarrior.us

The Michigan Lyme Disease Association: (888) 784-5963

Minnesota Lyme Associations: http://mnlyme.org

NatCapLyme: www.natcaplyme.org

New Jersey: www.lymenet.org

Open Eye Productions: www.openeyepictures.com; "Under Our Skin"

PA Lyme Resource Network: palyme.org

Southern Tier Lyme Support: Endicott, NY: www.southerntierlymesupport.org

Texas Lyme Disease Association: www.txlda.com

Ticked Off Foundation: www.tickedofffoundation.org

Vermont Lyme: vermontlyme.com

Wisconsin Lyme Network Home: https://wisconsinlymenetwork.org/

Wisconsin Support Groups - Wisconsin Lyme Network - Patients Site: www.wisconsinlymenetwork.org/patients/wisconsin-support-groups/

Supplement Companies

Brand Direct Heath: (866) 331-6440

Etain Health: (914) 437-7898
Lee Sillsby Compounding Pharmacy: (800) 918-8831
NutraMetix: (561) 745-2917
Researched Nutritional: (800)755-3402
Wellness Pharmacy: (800) 227-2627

Studies

https://www.Als-cure.com/als-lyme

https://www.Dr.Alan Mc Donald; "Alzheimer Borreliosis" www.alzheimerborreliosis.net

https://www.Shoemaker Study – "Surviving Mold" www.survivingmold.com/news/2013/03/new-dr-shoemaker-published-study-coming-to-surviving-mold

https://www.Lymestats.org

https://www.Norvect.no/230-peer-reviewed-studies-show-evidenv=ce-of-persistent-lyme-disease

https://www.ncbi.nlm.nih.gov/pubmed/3776998

Laboratories

Aramin Laboratories - www.arminlabs.com
Galaxy Laboratories - www.galaxylaboratories.com/products.html
Igenex - www.igenex.com
Lab Corp – www.labcorp.com
Quest Diagnostics - www.questdiagnostics.com

Fitness Facility

Edge Strength and Conditioning Gym
www.edgesyracuse.com

Author

Martha Conan: mconan@twcny.rr.com